Washington Irving

Old Christmas and Bracebridge Hall

Washington Irving

Old Christmas and Bracebridge Hall

ISBN/EAN: 9783337164515

Printed in Europe, USA, Canada, Australia, Japan

Cover: Foto ©Lupo / pixelio.de

More available books at **www.hansebooks.com**

OLD CHRISTMAS

AND

BRACEBRIDGE HALL

Old Christmas was first published with Randolph Caldecott's Illustrations in 1875 and Bracebridge Hall in 1876

OLD CHRISTMAS

AND

BRACEBRIDGE HALL

BY

WASHINGTON IRVING

ILLUSTRATED BY RANDOLPH CALDECOTT

NEW EDITION

London
MACMILLAN AND CO.
AND NEW YORK
1886

OLD CHRISTMAS

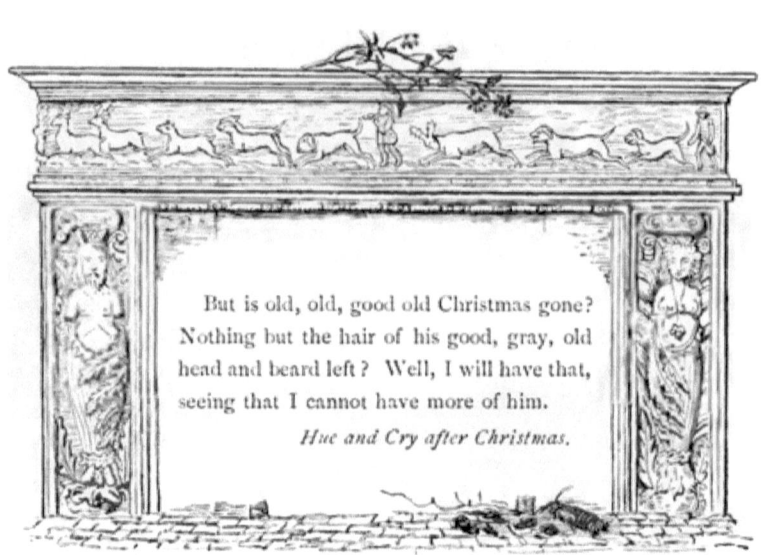

But is old, old, good old Christmas gone? Nothing but the hair of his good, gray, old head and beard left? Well, I will have that, seeing that I cannot have more of him.

Hue and Cry after Christmas.

BEFORE the remembrance of the good old times, so fast passing, should have entirely passed away, the present artist, R. Caldecott, and engraver, James D. Cooper, planned to illustrate Washington Irving's "Old Christmas" in this manner. Their primary idea was to carry out the principle of the Sketch Book, by incorporating the designs with the text. Throughout they have worked together and *con amore*. With what success the public must decide.

NOVEMBER 1875.

CONTENTS

	PAGE
CHRISTMAS	1
THE STAGE COACH	11
CHRISTMAS EVE	27
CHRISTMAS DAY	55
THE CHRISTMAS DINNER	85

DESIGNED BY RANDOLPH CALDECOTT,

AND

ARRANGED AND ENGRAVED BY J. D. COOPER.

	PAGE
TITLE-PAGE	
ANCIENT FIREPLACE	iv
HEADING TO PREFACE	v
HEADING TO CONTENTS	vii
TAILPIECE TO CONTENTS	vii
HEADING TO LIST OF ILLUSTRATIONS	ix
TAILPIECE TO LIST OF ILLUSTRATIONS	xiii
"THE POOR FROM THE GATES WERE NOT CHIDDEN"	xvi
HEADING TO CHRISTMAS	1
THE MOULDERING TOWER	1
CHRISTMAS ANTHEM IN CATHEDRAL	2
THE WANDERER'S RETURN	3
"NATURE LIES DESPOILED OF EVERY CHARM"	4

LIST OF ILLUSTRATIONS

	PAGE
"The Honest Face of Hospitality"	4
"The Shy Glance of Love"	5
Old Hall of Castle	5
The Great Oaken Gallery	6
The Waits	7
"And sit down Darkling and Repining"	9
The Stage Coach	13
The Three Schoolboys	14
The Old English Stage Coachman	15
"He throws down the Reins with something of an Air"	16
The Stable Imitators	17
The Public House	18
The Housemaid	18
The Smithy	19
"Now or never must Music be in tune"	20
The Country Maid	20
The Old Servant and Bantam	21
A Neat Country Seat	22
Inn Kitchen	23
The Recognition	24
The Post-chaise	29
The Lodge Gate	31
The Old Primitive Dame	33
"The Little Dogs and All"	34
The Old Mansion by Moonlight	36
Mistletoe	38
The Squire's Reception	38
The Family Party	40

LIST OF ILLUSTRATIONS

	PAGE
TOYS	41
THE YULE LOG	42
THE SQUIRE IN HIS HEREDITARY CHAIR	43
THE FAMILY PLATE	44
MASTER SIMON	45
YOUNG GIRL	45
HER MOTHER	45
THE OLD HARPER	47
MASTER SIMON DANCING	48
THE OXONIAN AND HIS MAIDEN AUNT	49
THE YOUNG OFFICER WITH HIS GUITAR	50
THE FAIR JULIA	52
ASLEEP	54
CHRISTMAS DAY	57
THE CHILDREN'S CAROL	58
ROBIN ON THE MOUNTAIN ASH	59
MASTER SIMON AS CLERK	60
BREAKFAST	61
VIEWING THE DOGS	62
MASTER SIMON GOING TO CHURCH	64
THE VILLAGE CHURCH	65
THE PARSON	66
REBUKING THE SEXTON	68
EFFIGY OF A WARRIOR	70
MASTER SIMON AT CHURCH	70
THE VILLAGE CHOIR	72
THE VILLAGE TAILOR	73
AN OLD CHORISTER	74

LIST OF ILLUSTRATIONS

	PAGE
The Sermon	75
Churchyard Greetings	77
Frosty Thraldom of Winter	78
Merry Old English Games	79
The Poor at Home	80
Village Antics	81
Tasting the Squire's Ale	82
The Wit of the Village	83
Coquettish Housemaid	83
Antique Sideboard	87
The Cook with the Rolling-Pin	88
The Warrior's Arms	88
The Christmas Dinner	90
"Flagons, Cans, Cups, Beakers, Goblets, Basins, and Ewers"	91
A High Roman Nose	92
The Parson said Grace	92
The Boar's Head	93
The Fat-headed Old Gentleman	95
Peacock Pie	95
The Wassail Bowl	97
The Squire's Toast	98
The Long-winded Joker	99
Long Stories	100
The Parson and the Pretty Milkmaid	100
Master Simon grows Maudlin	101
The Blue-Eyed Romp	103
The Parson's Tale	104

LIST OF ILLUSTRATIONS

xiii

	PAGE
The Sexton's Rebuff	105
The Crusader's Night Ride	106
Ancient Christmas and Dame Mince-Pie	108
Robin Hood and Maid Marian	108
The Minuet	109
Roast Beef, Plum Pudding, and Misrule	111
The Christmas Dance in Costume	112
"Chuckling and rubbing his Hands"	112
"Echoing back the Joviality of long-departed Years"	113
Retrospect	114

CHRISTMAS

A man might then behold
   At Christmas, in each hall
Good fires to curb the cold,
   And meat for great and small.
The neighbours were friendly bidden,
   And all had welcome true,
The poor from the gates were not chidden,
   When this old cap was new.

OLD SONG.

CHRISTMAS

THERE is nothing in England that exercises a more delightful spell over my imagination than the lingerings of the holiday customs and rural games of former times. They recall the pictures my fancy used to draw in the May morning of life, when as yet I only knew the world through books, and believed it to be all that poets had painted it; and they bring with them the flavour of those honest days of yore, in which, perhaps with equal fallacy, I am apt to think the world was more homebred, social, and joyous than at present. I regret to say that they are daily growing more and more faint, being gradually worn away by time, but still more obliterated by modern fashion. They resemble those picturesque morsels of Gothic architecture which we see crumbling

in various parts of the country, partly dilapidated by the waste of ages, and partly lost in the additions and alterations of latter days. Poetry, however, clings with cherishing fondness about the rural game and holiday revel, from which it has derived so many of its themes—as the ivy winds its rich foliage about the Gothic arch and mouldering tower, gratefully repaying their support by clasping together their tottering remains, and, as it were, embalming them in verdure.

Of all the old festivals, however, that of Christmas awakens the strongest and most heartfelt associations. There is a tone of solemn and sacred feeling that blends with our conviviality, and lifts the spirit to a state of hallowed and elevated enjoyment. The services of the church about this season are extremely tender and inspiring. They dwell on the beautiful story of the origin of our faith, and the pastoral scenes that accompanied its announcement. They gradually increase in fervour and pathos during the season of Advent, until they break forth in full jubilee on the morning that brought peace and good-will to men. I do not know a grander effect of music on the moral feelings than to hear the full choir and the pealing organ performing a Christmas anthem in a cathedral, and filling every part of the vast pile with triumphant harmony.

It is a beautiful arrangement, also, derived from days of yore, that this festival, which commemorates the announcement of the religion of peace and love, has been made the season for gathering together of family connections, and drawing closer again those bands of kindred hearts which the cares and pleasures and sorrows of the world are continually operating to cast loose; of calling back the children of a family who have launched forth in life, and wandered widely asunder, once more to assemble about the paternal hearth, that rallying-place of the affections, there to grow young and loving again among the endearing mementoes of childhood.

There is something in the very season of the year that gives a charm to the festivity of Christmas. At other times we derive a great portion of our pleasures from the mere beauties of nature. Our feelings sally forth and dissipate themselves over the sunny landscape, and we "live abroad and everywhere." The song of the bird, the murmur of the stream, the breathing fragrance of spring, the soft voluptuousness of summer, the golden pomp of autumn ; earth with its mantle of refreshing green, and heaven with its deep delicious blue and its cloudy magnificence, all fill us with mute but exquisite delight, and we revel in the luxury of mere sensation. But in the depth of winter, when nature lies despoiled of every charm, and wrapped in her shroud of sheeted snow, we turn for our

gratifications to moral sources. The dreariness and desolation of the landscape, the short gloomy days and darksome nights, while they circumscribe our wanderings, shut in our feelings also from rambling abroad, and make us more keenly disposed for the pleasures of the social circle. Our thoughts are more concentrated; our friendly sympathies more aroused. We feel more sensibly the charm of each other's society, and are brought more closely together by dependence on each other for enjoyment. Heart calleth unto heart; and we draw our pleasures from the deep wells of living kindness, which lie in the quiet recesses of our bosoms; and which, when resorted to, furnish forth the pure element of domestic felicity.

The pitchy gloom without makes the heart dilate on entering the room filled with the glow and warmth of the evening fire. The ruddy blaze diffuses an artificial summer and sunshine through the room, and lights up each countenance into a kindlier welcome. Where does the honest face of hospitality expand into a broader and more cordial smile—

where is the shy glance of love more sweetly eloquent—than by the winter fireside? and as the hollow blast of wintry wind rushes through the hall, claps the distant door, whistles about the casement, and rumbles down the chimney, what can be more grateful than that feeling of sober and sheltered security with which we look round upon the comfortable chamber and the scene of domestic hilarity?

The English, from the great prevalence of rural habits throughout every class of society, have always been fond of those festivals and holidays which agreeably interrupt the stillness of country life; and they were, in former days, particularly observant of the religious and social rites of Christmas. It is inspiring to read even the dry details which some antiquarians have given of the quaint humours, the burlesque pageants, the complete abandonment to mirth and good-fellowship, with which this festival was celebrated. It seemed to throw open every door, and unlock every heart. It brought the peasant and the peer together, and blended all ranks in one warm generous flow of joy and kindness. The old halls of castles and manor-houses resounded with the harp and the Christmas carol, and their ample boards groaned under the weight of hospitality. Even the poorest cottage welcomed the festive season with green decorations of bay and holly —the cheerful fire glanced its rays through the lattice, inviting the passenger to raise the latch, and join the gossip knot huddled round the hearth, beguiling the long evening with legendary jokes and oft-told Christmas tales.

One of the least pleasing effects of modern refinement is the havoc it has made among the hearty old holiday customs. It has completely taken off the sharp touchings and spirited

reliefs of these embellishments of life, and has worn down society into a more smooth and polished, but certainly a less characteristic surface. Many of the games and ceremonials of Christmas have entirely disappeared, and, like the sherris sack of old Falstaff, are become matters of speculation and dispute among commentators. They flourished in times full of spirit and lustihood, when men enjoyed life roughly, but heartily and vigorously; times wild and picturesque, which have furnished poetry with its richest materials, and the drama with its most attractive variety of characters and manners. The world has become more worldly. There is more of dissipation, and less of enjoyment. Pleasure has expanded into a broader, but a shallower stream, and has forsaken many of those deep and quiet channels where it flowed sweetly through the calm bosom of domestic life. Society has acquired a more enlightened and elegant tone; but it has lost many of its strong local peculiarities, its home-bred feelings, its honest fireside delights. The traditionary customs of golden-hearted antiquity, its feudal hospitalities, and lordly wassailings, have passed away with the baronial castles and stately manor-houses in which they were celebrated. They comported with the shadowy hall, the great oaken gallery, and the tapestried parlour, but are unfitted to the light showy saloons and gay drawing-rooms of the modern villa.

Shorn, however, as it is, of its ancient and festive honours, Christmas is still a period of delightful excitement in England. It is gratifying to see that home feeling completely aroused which seems to hold so powerful a place in every English bosom. The preparations making on every side for the social board that is again to unite friends and kindred; the presents of good cheer passing and repassing, those tokens of regard, and quickeners of kind feelings; the evergreens distributed about houses and churches, emblems of peace and gladness;

all these have the most pleasing effect in producing fond associations, and kindling benevolent sympathies. Even the sound of the waits, rude as may be their minstrelsy, breaks upon the mid-watches of a winter night with the effect of perfect harmony. As I have been awakened by them in that still and solemn hour, "when deep sleep falleth upon man," I have listened with a hushed delight, and, connecting them with the sacred and joyous occasion, have almost fancied them into another celestial choir, announcing peace and good-will to mankind.

How delightfully the imagination, when wrought upon by these moral influences, turns everything to melody and beauty: The very crowing of the cock, who is sometimes heard in the profound repose of the country, "telling the night watches to his feathery dames," was thought by the common people to announce the approach of this sacred festival:—

> Some say that ever 'gainst that season comes
> Wherein our Saviour's birth is celebrated,
> This bird of dawning singeth all night long;
> And then, they say, no spirit dares stir abroad;
> The nights are wholesome—then no planets strike,
> No fairy takes, no witch hath power to charm,
> So hallow'd and so gracious is the time.

Amidst the general call to happiness, the bustle of the spirits, and stir of the affections, which prevail at this period, what bosom can remain insensible? It is, indeed, the season of regenerated feeling—the season for kindling, not merely the fire of hospitality in the hall, but the genial flame of charity in the heart.

The scene of early love again rises green to memory beyond the sterile waste of years; and the idea of home, fraught with the fragrance of home-dwelling joys, reanimates the drooping spirit,—as the Arabian breeze will sometimes waft the freshness of the distant fields to the weary pilgrim of the desert.

Stranger and sojourner as I am in the land—though for me no social hearth may blaze, no hospitable roof throw open its doors, nor the warm grasp of friendship welcome me at the threshold—yet I feel the influence of the season beaming into my soul from the happy looks of those around me. Surely happiness is reflective, like the light of heaven; and every countenance, bright with smiles, and glowing with innocent enjoyment, is a mirror transmitting to others the rays of a supreme and ever-shining benevolence. He who can turn churlishly away from contemplating the felicity of his fellow-beings, and sit down darkling and repining in his loneliness when all around is joyful, may have his moments of strong excitement and selfish gratification, but he wants the genial and social sympathies which constitute the charm of a merry Christmas.

The Stage Coach

Omne benè
Sine pœnâ
Tempus est ludendi:
Venit hora,
Absque morâ.
Libros deponendi.
Old Holiday School Song.

THE STAGE COACH

IN the preceding paper I have made some general observavations on the Christmas festivities of England, and am tempted to illustrate them by some anecdotes of a Christmas passed in the country; in perusing which, I would most courteously invite my reader to lay aside the austerity of wisdom, and to put on that genuine holiday spirit which is tolerant of folly, and anxious only for amusement. In the course of a December tour in Yorkshire, I rode for a long distance in one of the public coaches, on the day preceding Christmas. The coach was crowded, both inside and out, with passengers, who, by their talk, seemed principally bound to the mansions of relations or friends to eat the Christmas dinner. It was loaded also with hampers of game, and baskets and boxes of delicacies; and hares hung dangling their long ears about the coachman's box,—presents from distant friends for the impending feast. I had three fine rosy-cheeked schoolboys for my fellow-passengers inside, full of the buxom health and manly spirit which I have observed in the children of this country. They were returning home for the holidays in high glee, and promising themselves a world of enjoyment. It was delightful to hear the gigantic plans of pleasure of the little rogues, and the impracticable feats they were to perform during their six weeks' emancipation from the abhorred thraldom of book, birch, and pedagogue. They were full of

anticipations of the meeting with the family and household, down to the very cat and dog; and of the joy they were to give their little sisters by the presents with which their pockets were crammed; but the meeting to which they seemed to look forward with the greatest impatience was with Bantam, which I found to be a pony, and, according to their talk, possessed of more virtues than any steed since the days of Bucephalus. How he could trot! how he could run! and then such leaps as he would take—there was not a hedge in the whole country that he could not clear.

They were under the particular guardianship of the coachman, to whom, whenever an opportunity presented, they addressed a host of questions, and pronounced him one of the best fellows in the whole world. Indeed, I could not but notice the more than ordinary air of bustle and importance of the coachman, who wore his hat a little on one side, and had a large bunch of Christmas greens stuck in the button-hole of his coat. He is always a personage full of mighty care and business, but he is particularly so during this season, having so many commissions to execute in consequence of the great interchange of presents. And here, perhaps, it may not be unacceptable to my untravelled readers, to have a sketch that may serve as a general representation of this very numerous and important class of functionaries, who have a dress, a manner, a language, an air, peculiar to themselves, and prevalent throughout the fraternity; so that wherever an English stage-coachman may be seen, he cannot be mistaken for one of any other craft or mystery.

He has commonly a broad, full face, curiously mottled with red, as if the blood had been forced by hard feeding into every vessel of the skin; he is swelled into jolly dimensions by frequent potations of malt liquors, and his bulk is still further increased by a multiplicity of coats, in which he is buried like a cauliflower, the upper one reaching to his heels. He wears a broad-brimmed, low-crowned hat; a huge roll of coloured handkerchief about his neck, knowingly knotted and tucked in at the bosom; and has in summertime a large bouquet of flowers in his button-hole; the present, most probably, of some enamoured country lass. His waistcoat is commonly of some bright colour, striped; and his small-clothes extend far below the  knees, to meet a pair of jockey boots which reach about half-way up his legs. All this costume is maintained with much precision; he has a pride in having his clothes of excellent materials; and, notwithstanding the seeming grossness of his appearance, there is still discernible that neatness and propriety of person which is almost inherent in an Englishman. He enjoys great consequence and consideration along the road; has frequent conferences with the village housewives, who look upon him as a man of great trust and dependence; and he seems to have a good understanding with every bright-eyed country lass. The moment he arrives where the horses are to be changed, he throws down the reins with something of an air, and abandons the cattle to the care of the hostler; his duty being merely to drive from one stage to another. When off

the box, his hands are thrust in the pockets of his greatcoat, and he rolls about the inn-yard with an air of the most absolute lordliness. Here he is generally surrounded by an admiring throng of hostlers, stable-boys, shoeblacks, and those nameless hangers-on that infest inns and taverns, and run errands, and do all kinds of odd jobs, for the privilege of battening on the drippings of the kitchen and the leakage of the tap-room. These all look up to him as to an oracle; treasure up his cant phrases; echo his opinions about horses and other topics of jockey lore; and, above all, endeavour to imitate his air and carriage. Every ragamuffin that has a coat to his back thrusts

his hands in the pockets, rolls in his gait, talks slang, and is an embryo Coachey.

Perhaps it might be owing to the pleasing serenity that reigned in my own mind, that I fancied I saw cheerfulness in every countenance throughout the journey. A stage coach, however, carries animation always with it, and puts the world in motion as it whirls along. The horn sounded at the entrance of a village produces a general bustle. Some hasten forth to meet friends; some with bundles and bandboxes to secure places, and in the hurry of the moment can hardly take leave of the group that accompanies them. In the meantime, the coachman has a world of small commissions to execute. Sometimes he delivers a hare or pheasant; sometimes jerks a small parcel or newspaper to the door of a public-house; and sometimes, with knowing leer and words of sly import, hands to some half-blushing, half-laughing housemaid an odd-shaped billet-doux from some rustic admirer.

As the coach rattles through the village, every one runs to the window, and you have glances on every side of fresh country faces, and blooming giggling girls. At the corners are assembled juntas of village idlers and wise men, who take their stations there for the important purpose of seeing company pass; but the sagest knot is generally at the blacksmith's, to whom the passing of the coach is an event fruitful of much speculation. The smith, with the horse's heel in his lap, pauses as the vehicle

whirls by; the Cyclops round the anvil suspend their ringing hammers, and suffer the iron to grow cool; and the sooty spectre in brown paper cap, labouring at the bellows, leans on the handle for a moment, and permits the asthmatic engine

to heave a long-drawn sigh, while he glares through the murky smoke and sulphureous gleams of the smithy.

Perhaps the impending holiday might have given a more than usual animation to the country, for it seemed to me as if everybody was in good looks and good spirits. Game, poultry, and other luxuries of the table, were in brisk circulation in the villages; the grocers', butchers', and fruiterers' shops were thronged with customers. The housewives were stirring briskly about, putting their dwellings in order; and the glossy branches

of holly, with their bright red berries, began to appear at the windows. The scene brought to mind an old writer's account of Christmas preparations:—" Now capons and hens, besides turkeys, geese, and ducks; with beef and mutton—must all die;

for in twelve days a multitude of people will not be fed with a little. Now plums and spice, sugar and honey, square it among pies and broth. Now or never must music be in tune, for the youth must dance and sing to get them a heat, while the aged sit by the fire. The country maid leaves half her market, and must be sent again, if she forgets a pack of cards on Christmas eve. Great is the contention of Holly and Ivy, whether master or dame wears the breeches. Dice and cards benefit the butler; and if the cook do not lack wit, he will sweetly lick his fingers."

I was roused from this fit of luxurious meditation by a shout from my little travelling companions. They had been looking out of the coach-windows for the last few miles, recognising every tree and cottage as they approached home, and now there was a general burst of joy—"There's John! and there's old Carlo! and there's Bantam!" cried the happy little rogues, clapping their hands.

At the end of a lane there was an old sober-looking servant in livery waiting for them: he was accompanied by a superannuated pointer, and by the redoubtable Bantam, a little old rat of a pony, with a shaggy mane and long rusty tail, who stood dozing quietly by the roadside, little dreaming of the bustling times that awaited him.

I was pleased to see the fondness with which the little fellows leaped about the steady old footman, and hugged the pointer, who wriggled his whole body for joy. But Bantam was the great object of interest; all wanted to mount at once; and it was with some difficulty that John arranged that they should ride by turns, and the eldest should ride first.

Off they set at last; one on the pony, with the dog bounding and barking before him, and the others holding John's hands; both talking at once, and overpowering him by questions about home, and with school anecdotes. I looked after them with a feeling in which I do not know whether pleasure or melancholy predominated: for I was reminded of those days when, like them, I had neither known care nor sorrow, and a holiday was the summit of earthly felicity. We stopped a few moments afterwards to water the horses, and on resuming our route, a turn of the road brought us in sight of a neat country-seat. I could just distinguish the forms of a lady and two young girls in the portico, and I saw my little comrades, with Bantam, Carlo, and old John, trooping along the carriage road.

I leaned out of the coach-window, in hopes of witnessing the happy meeting, but a grove of trees shut it from my sight.

In the evening we reached a village where I had determined to pass the night. As we drove into the great gateway of the inn, I saw on one side the light of a rousing kitchen fire, beaming through a window. I entered, and admired, for the hundredth time, that picture of convenience, neatness, and broad honest enjoyment, the kitchen of an English inn. It was of spacious dimensions, hung round with copper and tin vessels highly polished, and decorated here and there with a Christmas green. Hams, tongues, and flitches of bacon, were suspended from the ceiling; a smoke-jack made its ceaseless clanking beside the fireplace, and a clock ticked in one corner. A well-scoured deal table extended along one side of the kitchen, with a cold round of beef, and other hearty viands upon it, over which two foaming tankards of ale seemed mounting guard. Travellers of inferior order were preparing to attack this stout

repast, while others sat smoking and gossiping over their ale on two high-backed oaken seats beside the fire. Trim housemaids were hurrying backwards and forwards under the directions of a fresh, bustling landlady; but still seizing an occasional moment to exchange a flippant word, and have a rallying laugh, with the group round the fire.

The scene completely realised Poor Robin's humble idea of the comforts of mid-winter.

> Now trees their leafy hats do bare,
> To reverence Winter's silver hair;
> A handsome hostess, merry host,
> A pot of ale now and a toast,
> Tobacco and a good coal fire,
> Are things this season doth require.*

I had not been long at the inn when a post-chaise drove up to the door. A young gentleman stepped out, and by the

light of the lamps I caught a glimpse of a countenance which I thought I knew. I moved forward to get a nearer view, when his eye caught mine. I was not mistaken; it was Frank Bracebridge, a sprightly good-humoured young fellow, with whom I had once travelled on the Continent. Our meeting was extremely cordial; for the countenance of an old fellow-traveller always brings up the recollection of a thousand

* Poor Robin's Almanack, 1684.

pleasant scenes, odd adventures, and excellent jokes. To discuss all these in a transient interview at an inn was impossible; and finding that I was not pressed for time, and was merely making a tour of observation, he insisted that I should give him a day or two at his father's country-seat, to which he was going to pass the holidays, and which lay at a few miles' distance. "It is better than eating a solitary Christmas dinner at an inn," said he; "and I can assure you of a hearty welcome in something of the old-fashion style." His reasoning was cogent; and I must confess the preparation I had seen for universal festivity and social enjoyment had made me feel a little impatient of my loneliness. I closed, therefore, at once with his invitation: the chaise drove up to the door; and in a few moments I was on my way to the family mansion of the Bracebridges.

CHRISTMAS EVE

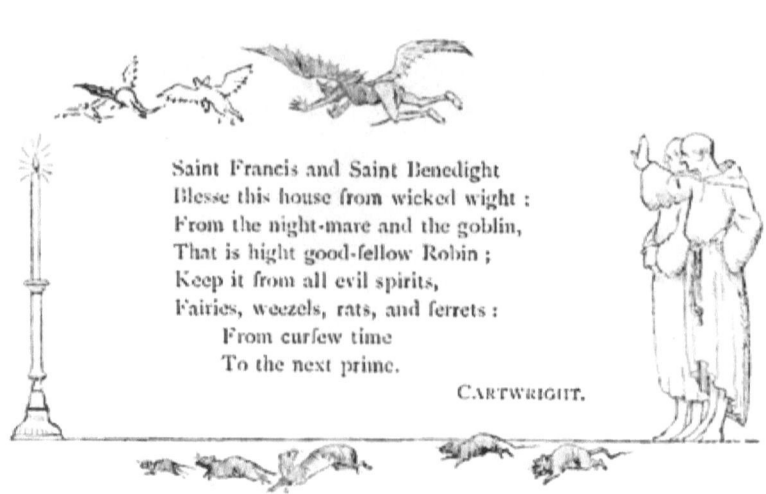

Saint Francis and Saint Benedight
Blesse this house from wicked wight:
From the night-mare and the goblin,
That is hight good-fellow Robin;
Keep it from all evil spirits,
Fairies, weezels, rats, and ferrets:
    From curfew time
    To the next prime.

CARTWRIGHT.

CHRISTMAS EVE

IT was a brilliant moonlight night, but extremely cold; our chaise whirled rapidly over the frozen ground; the post-boy smacked his whip incessantly, and a part of the time his horses were on a gallop. "He knows where he is going," said my companion, laughing, "and is eager to arrive in time for some of the merriment and good cheer of the servants' hall. My father, you must know, is a bigoted devotee of the old school, and prides himself upon keeping up something of old English hospitality. He is a tolerable specimen of what you will rarely meet with nowadays in its purity, the old English country gentleman; for our men of fortune spend so much of their time in town, and fashion is carried so much into the country, that the strong rich peculiarities of ancient rural life are almost polished away. My father, however, from early years, took honest Peacham* for his text book, instead of Chesterfield: he determined, in his own mind, that there was no condition more truly honourable and enviable than that

* Peacham's Complete Gentleman, 1622.

of a country gentleman on his paternal lands, and, therefore, passes the whole of his time on his estate. He is a strenuous advocate for the revival of the old rural games and holiday observances, and is deeply read in the writers, ancient and modern, who have treated on the subject. Indeed, his favourite range of reading is among the authors who flourished at least two centuries since; who, he insists, wrote and thought more like true Englishmen than any of their successors. He even regrets sometimes that he had not been born a few centuries earlier, when England was itself, and had its peculiar manners and customs. As he lives at some distance from the main road, in rather a lonely part of the country, without any rival gentry near him, he has that most enviable of all blessings to an Englishman, an opportunity of indulging the bent of his own humour without molestation. Being representative of the oldest family in the neighbourhood, and a great part of the peasantry being his tenants, he is much looked up to, and, in general, is known simply by the appellation of 'The Squire;' a title which has been accorded to the head of the family since time immemorial. I think it best to give you these hints about my worthy old father, to prepare you for any little eccentricities that might otherwise appear absurd."

We had passed for some time along the wall of a park, and at length the chaise stopped at the gate. It was in a heavy magnificent old style, of iron bars, fancifully wrought at top into flourishes and flowers. The huge square columns that supported the gate were surmounted by the family crest. Close adjoining was the porter's lodge, sheltered under dark fir-trees, and almost buried in shrubbery.

The post-boy rang a large porter's bell, which resounded through the still frosty air, and was answered by the distant barking of dogs, with which the mansion house seemed garrisoned. An old woman immediately appeared at the gate. As the moonlight fell strongly upon her, I had a full view of a

'It was in a heavy magnificent old style, of iron bars, fancifully wrought at top into flourishes and flowers.'

little primitive dame, dressed very much in the antique taste, with a neat kerchief and stomacher, and her silver hair peeping from under a cap of snowy whiteness. She came curtseying forth, with many expressions of simple joy at seeing her young master. Her husband, it seems, was up at the house keeping Christmas eve in the servants' hall; they could not do without him, as he was the best hand at a song and story in the household.

My friend proposed that we should alight and walk through the park to the hall, which was at no great distance, while the chaise should follow on. Our road wound through a noble avenue of trees, among the naked branches of which the moon glittered as she rolled through the deep vault of a cloudless sky. The lawn beyond was sheeted with a slight covering of snow, which here and there sparkled as the moonbeams caught a frosty crystal; and at a distance might be seen a thin transparent vapour, stealing up from the low grounds, and threatening gradually to shroud the landscape.

My companion looked round him with transport:—" How often," said he, " have I scampered up this avenue, on returning home on school vacations! How often have I played under these trees when a boy! I feel a degree of filial reverence for them, as we look up to those who have cherished us in childhood. My father was always scrupulous in exacting our holidays and having us around him on family festivals. He used to direct and superintend our games with the strictness that some parents do the studies of their children. He was very particular that we should play the old English games according to their original form; and consulted old books for precedent and authority for every 'merrie disport;' yet I assure you there never was pedantry so delightful. It was the policy of the good old gentleman to make his children feel that home was the happiest place in the world; and I value this delicious home-feeling as one of the choicest gifts a parent can bestow."

We were interrupted by the clangour of a troop of dogs of all sorts and sizes, " mongrel, puppy, whelp, and hound, and

curs of low degree," that, disturbed by the ringing of the porter's bell, and the rattling of the chaise, came bounding, open-mouthed, across the lawn.

——" The little dogs and all,
Tray, Blanch, and Sweetheart—see they bark at me !"

cried Bracebridge, laughing. At the sound of his voice the bark was changed into a yelp of delight, and in a moment he

'The old family mansion, partly thrown in deep shadow, and partly lit up by the cold moonshine.'

was surrounded and almost overpowered by the caresses of the faithful animals.

We had now come in full view of the old family mansion, partly thrown in deep shadow, and partly lit up by the cold moonshine. It was an irregular building of some magnitude, and seemed to be of the architecture of different periods. One wing was evidently very ancient, with heavy stone-shafted bow windows jutting out and overrun with ivy, from among the foliage of which the small diamond-shaped panes of glass glittered with the moonbeams. The rest of the house was in the French taste of Charles the Second's time, having been repaired and altered, as my friend told me, by one of his ancestors, who returned with that monarch at the Restoration. The grounds about the house were laid out in the old formal manner of artificial flower-beds, clipped shrubberies, raised terraces, and heavy stone balustrades, ornamented with urns, a leaden statue or two, and a jet of water. The old gentleman, I was told, was extremely careful to preserve this obsolete finery in all its original state. He admired this fashion in gardening; it had an air of magnificence, was courtly and noble, and befitting good old family style. The boasted imitation of nature in modern gardening had sprung up with modern republican notions, but did not suit a monarchical government; it smacked of the levelling system.—I could not help smiling at this introduction of politics into gardening, though I expressed some apprehension that I should find the old gentleman rather intolerant in his creed.—Frank assured me, however, that it was almost the only instance in which he had ever heard his father meddle with politics; and he believed that he had got this notion from a member of parliament who once passed a few weeks with him. The Squire was glad of any argument to defend his clipped yew-trees and formal terraces, which had been occasionally attacked by modern landscape-gardeners.

As we approached the house, we heard the sound of music, and now and then a burst of laughter from one end of the building. This, Bracebridge said, must proceed from the servants' hall, where a great deal of revelry was permitted, and even encouraged, by the Squire throughout the twelve days of Christmas, provided everything was done conformably to ancient usage. Here were kept up the old games of hoodman blind, shoe the wild mare, hot cockles, steal the white loaf, bob apple, and snap-dragon: the Yule log and Christmas candle were regularly burnt, and the mistletoe, with its white berries, hung up, to the imminent peril of all the pretty housemaids.*

So intent were the servants upon their sports, that we had to ring repeatedly before we could make ourselves heard. On our arrival being

* See Note A.

'The company, which was assembled in a large old-fashioned hall.'

announced, the Squire came out to receive us, accompanied by his two other sons; one a young officer in the army, home on leave of absence; the other an Oxonian, just from the university. The Squire was a fine, healthy-looking old gentleman, with silver hair curling lightly round an open florid countenance: in which a physiognomist, with the advantage, like myself, of a previous hint or two, might discover a singular mixture of whim and benevolence.

The family meeting was warm and affectionate; as the evening was far advanced, the Squire would not permit us to change our travelling dresses, but ushered us at once to the company, which was assembled in a large old-fashioned hall. It was composed of different branches of a numerous family connection, where there were the usual proportion of old uncles and aunts, comfortably married dames, superannuated spinsters, blooming country cousins, half-fledged striplings, and bright-eyed boarding-school hoydens. They were variously occupied: some at a round game of cards; others conversing around the fireplace; at one end of the hall was a group of the young

folks, some nearly grown up, others of a more tender and budding age, fully engrossed by a merry game; and a profusion of wooden horses, penny trumpets, and tattered dolls, about the floor, showed traces of a troop of little fairy beings, who, having frolicked through a happy day, had been carried off to slumber through a peaceful night. While the mutual greetings were going on between Bracebridge and his relatives, I had time to scan the apartment. I have called it a hall,

for so it had certainly been in old times, and the Squire had evidently endeavoured to restore it to something of its primitive state. Over the heavy projecting fireplace was suspended a picture of a warrior in armour, standing by a white horse, and on the opposite wall hung helmet, buckler, and lance. At one end an enormous pair of antlers were inserted in the wall, the branches serving as hooks on which to suspend hats whips, and spurs; and in the corners of the apartment were fowling-pieces, fishing rods, and other sporting implements. The furniture was of the cumbrous workmanship of former days, though some articles of modern convenience had been added, and the oaken floor had been carpeted; so that the whole presented an odd mixture of parlour and hall.

The grate had been removed from the wide overwhelming fireplace, to make way for a fire of wood, in the midst of which was an enormous log glowing and blazing, and sending forth a vast volume of light and heat; this I understood was the Yule-log, which the Squire was particular in having brought in and illumined on a Christmas eve, according to ancient custom.*

It was really delightful to see the old Squire seated in his hereditary elbow-chair by the hospitable fireside of his ancestors, and looking around him like the sun of a system, beaming warmth and gladness to every heart. Even the very dog that lay stretched at his feet, as he lazily shifted his position and yawned, would look fondly up in his master's face, wag his tail against the floor, and stretch himself again to sleep, confident of kindness  and protection. There is an emanation from the heart in genuine hospitality which cannot be described, but is immediately felt, and puts the stranger at once at his ease. I had not been seated many minutes by the comfortable hearth of the worthy cavalier before I found myself as much at home

* See Note B.

as if I had been one of the family. Supper was announced shortly after our arrival. It was served up in a spacious oaken chamber, the panels of which shone with wax, and around which were several family portraits decorated with holly and ivy. Beside the accustomed lights, two great wax tapers, called Christmas candles, wreathed with greens, were placed

on a highly polished buffet among the family plate. The table was abundantly spread with substantial fare; but the Squire made his supper of frumenty, a dish made of wheat cakes boiled in milk with rich spices, being a standing dish in old times for Christmas eve. I was happy to find my old friend, minced-pie, in the retinue of the feast; and finding him to be perfectly orthodox, and that I need not be ashamed of my predilection, I greeted him with all the warmth wherewith we usually greet an old and very genteel acquaintance.

The mirth of the company was greatly promoted by the humours of an eccentric personage whom Mr. Bracebridge always addressed with the quaint appellation of Master Simon. He was a tight, brisk little man, with the air of an arrant old bachelor. His nose was shaped like the bill of a parrot; his face  slightly pitted with the small-pox, with a dry perpetual bloom on it, like a frost-bitten leaf in autumn. He had an eye of great quickness and vivacity, with a drollery and lurking waggery of expression that was irresistible. He was evidently the wit of the family, dealing very much in sly jokes and innuendoes with the ladies, and making infinite merriment by harpings upon old themes; which, unfortunately, my ignorance of the family chronicles did not permit me to enjoy. It seemed to be his

great delight during supper to keep a young girl next him in a continual agony of stifled laughter, in spite of her awe of the reproving looks of her mother, who sat opposite. Indeed, he was the idol of the younger part of the company, who laughed at everything he said or did, and at every turn of his countenance. I could not wonder at it; for he must have been a miracle of accomplishments in their eyes. He could imitate Punch and Judy; make an old woman of his hand, with the assistance of a burnt cork and pocket-handkerchief; and cut an orange into such a ludicrous caricature, that the young folks were ready to die with laughing.

I was let briefly into his history by Frank Bracebridge. He was an old bachelor of a small independent income, which by careful management was sufficient for all his wants. He revolved through the family system like a vagrant comet in its orbit; sometimes visiting one branch, and sometimes another quite remote; as is often the case with gentlemen of extensive connections and small fortunes in England. He had a chirping, buoyant disposition, always enjoying the present moment; and his frequent change of scene and company prevented his acquiring those rusty unaccommodating habits with which old bachelors are so uncharitably charged. He was a complete family chronicle, being versed in the genealogy, history, and intermarriages of the whole house of Bracebridge, which made him a great favourite with the old folks; he was a beau of all the elder ladies and superannuated spinsters, among whom he was habitually considered rather a young fellow, and he was a master of the revels among the children; so that there was not a more popular being in the sphere in which he moved than Mr. Simon Bracebridge. Of late years he had resided almost entirely with the Squire, to whom he had become a factotum, and whom he particularly delighted by jumping with his humour in respect to old times, and by having a scrap of an old song to suit every occasion. We had presently a specimen of his last-mentioned talent; for no sooner was supper removed, and spiced wines and other beverages peculiar to the season introduced, than Master Simon was called on for a good old Christmas song. He bethought himself for a moment, and then, with a sparkle of the eye, and a voice that was by no means bad, excepting that it ran occasionally into a falsetto, like the notes of a split reed, he quavered forth a quaint old ditty,—

> "Now Christmas is come,
>   Let us beat up the drum,
> And call all our neighbours together :
>   And when they appear,
>   Let us make them such cheer,
> As will keep out the wind and the weather," etc.

The supper had disposed every one to gaiety, and an old harper was summoned from the servants' hall, where he had been strumming all the evening, and to all appearance comforting himself with some of the Squire's home-brewed. He was a kind of hanger-on, I was told, of the establishment, and though ostensibly a resident of the village, was oftener to be found in the Squire's kitchen than his own home, the old gentleman being fond of the sound of "harp in hall."

The dance, like most dances after supper, was a merry one ; some of the older folks joined in it, and the Squire himself figured down several couples with a partner with whom he affirmed he had danced at every Christmas for nearly half-a-century. Master Simon, who seemed to be a kind of connecting link between the old times and the new, and to be withal a little antiquated in the taste of his accomplishments, evidently piqued himself on his dancing, and was endeavouring to gain credit by the heel and toe, rigadoon, and other graces of the ancient school; but he had unluckily assorted himself with a little romping girl from boarding-school, who, by her wild vivacity, kept him continually on the stretch, and defeated

all his sober attempts at elegance;—such are the ill-assorted matches to which antique gentlemen are unfortunately prone!

The young Oxonian, on the contrary, had led out one of his maiden aunts, on whom the rogue played a thousand little knaveries with impunity; he was full of practical jokes, and his delight was to tease his aunts and cousins; yet, like all madcap youngsters, he was a universal favourite among the women. The most interesting couple in the dance was the young officer and a ward of the Squire's, a beautiful blushing girl of seventeen. From several shy glances which I had noticed in the course of the evening, I suspected there was a little kindness growing up between them; and, indeed, the young soldier was just the hero to captivate a romantic girl.

He was tall, slender, and handsome, and like most young British officers of late years, had picked up various small accomplishments on the Continent—he could talk French and Italian—draw landscapes, sing very tolerably—dance divinely; but, above all, he had been wounded at Waterloo:—what girl of seventeen, well read in poetry and romance, could resist such a mirror of chivalry and perfection!

E

The moment the dance was over, he caught up a guitar, and lolling against the old marble fireplace, in an attitude which I am half inclined to suspect was studied, began the little French air of the Troubadour. The Squire, however, exclaimed against having anything on Christmas eve but good old English: upon

which the young minstrel, casting up his eye for a moment, as if in an effort of memory, struck into another strain, and, with a charming air of gallantry, gave Herrick's 'Night-Piece to Julia:"—

"Her eyes the glow-worm lend thee.
　The shooting stars attend thee,
　　And the elves also,
　　Whose little eyes glow
　Like the sparks of fire, befriend thee.

'Indeed, so great was her indifference, that she was amusing herself with plucking to pieces a choice bouquet of hot-house flowers.'

No Will-o'-the-Wisp mislight thee:
Nor snake or glow-worm bite thee;
  But on, on thy way,
  Not making a stay,
Since ghost there is none to affright thee.

Then let not the dark thee cumber;
What though the moon does slumber,
  The stars of the night
  Will lend thee their light,
Like tapers clear without number.

Then, Julia, let me woo thee,
Thus, thus to come unto me;
  And when I shall meet
  Thy silvery feet,
My soul I'll pour into thee."

The song might have been intended in compliment to the fair Julia, for so I found his partner was called, or it might not; she, however, was certainly unconscious of any such application, for she never looked at the singer, but kept her eyes cast upon the floor. Her face was suffused, it is true, with a beautiful blush, and there was a gentle heaving of the bosom, but all that was doubtless caused by the exercise of the dance; indeed, so great was her indifference, that she was amusing herself with plucking to pieces a choice bouquet of hot-house flowers, and by the time the song was concluded, the nosegay lay in ruins on the floor. The party now broke up for the night with the kind-hearted old custom of shaking hands. As I passed through the hall, on the way to my chamber, the dying embers of the *Yule-clog* still sent forth a dusky glow; and had it not been the season when "no spirit dares stir abroad," I should have been half tempted to steal from my room at midnight, and peep whether the fairies might not be at their revels about the hearth. My chamber was in the old part of the mansion, the ponderous furniture of which might have been fabricated in the days of the giants. The room was panelled with cornices of heavy carved-work, in which flowers and grotesque faces were strangely intermingled; and a row of black-looking portraits stared mournfully at me from the walls. The bed was of rich though faded damask, with a lofty tester, and stood in a niche opposite a bow-window. I had scarcely got into bed when a strain of music seemed to break forth in the air just below the window. I listened, and found it proceeded from a band, which I concluded to be the waits from some neighbouring village. They went round the house, playing under the windows. I drew aside the curtains, to hear them more distinctly. The moonbeams fell through the upper part of the casement, partially lighting up the antiquated apartment. The sounds, as they receded, became more soft and aërial, and seemed to accord with quiet and moonlight. I listened and listened— they became more and more tender and remote, and, as they gradually died away, my head sank upon the pillow and I fell asleep.

Christmas Day

Dark and dull night, flie hence away,
And give the honour to this day
That sees December turn'd to May.
  *   *   *
Why does the chilling winter's morne
Smile like a field beset with corn?
Or smell like to a meade new-shorne,
Thus on the sudden?— Come and see
The cause why things thus fragrant be.

HERRICK.

CHRISTMAS DAY

WHEN I awoke the next morning, it seemed as if all the events of the preceding evening had been a dream, and nothing but the identity of the ancient chamber convinced me of their reality. While I lay musing on my pillow, I heard the sound of little feet pattering outside of the door, and a whispering consultation. Presently a choir of small voices chanted forth an old Christmas carol, the burden of which was,

> Rejoice, our Saviour he was born
> On Christmas Day in the morning.

I rose softly, slipped on my clothes, opened the door suddenly, and beheld one of the most beautiful little fairy groups that a painter could imagine. It consisted of a boy and two girls, the eldest not more than six, and lovely as seraphs. They were going the rounds of the house, and singing at every chamber-door; but my sudden appearance frightened them into mute bashfulness. They remained for a moment playing on their lips with their fingers, and now and

then stealing a shy glance, from under their eyebrows, until, as if by one impulse, they scampered away, and as they turned an angle of the gallery, I heard them laughing in triumph at their escape.

Everything conspired to produce kind and happy feelings in this stronghold of old-fashioned hospitality. The window of my chamber looked out upon what in summer would have been a beautiful landscape. There was a sloping lawn, a fine stream winding at the foot of it, and a tract of park beyond, with noble clumps of trees, and herds of deer. At a distance was a neat hamlet, with the smoke from the cottage chimneys hanging over it; and a church with its dark spire in strong relief against the clear cold sky. The house was surrounded with evergreens, according to the English custom, which would have given almost an appearance of summer; but the morning was extremely frosty; the light vapour of the preceding evening had been precipitated by the cold, and covered all the trees and every blade of grass with its fine crystallisations. The rays of a bright morning sun had a dazzling effect among the glittering foliage. A robin, perched upon the top of a mountain-ash that hung its clusters of red berries just before my window, was basking himself in the sunshine, and piping a few querulous notes; and a peacock was displaying all the glories of his train, and strutting with the pride and gravity of a Spanish grandee on the terrace-walk below.

I had scarcely dressed myself, when a servant appeared to invite me to family prayers. He showed me the way to a small chapel in the old wing of the house, where I found the principal part of the family already assembled in a kind of gallery, furnished with cushions, hassocks, and large prayer-books; the servants were seated on benches below. The old gentleman read prayers from a desk in front of the gallery, and Master Simon acted as clerk, and made the responses; and I must do him

the justice to say that he acquitted himself with great gravity and decorum.

The service was followed by a Christmas carol, which Mr. Bracebridge himself had constructed from a poem of his favourite author, Herrick; and it had been adapted to an old church melody by Master Simon. As there were several good voices among the household, the effect was extremely pleasing; but I was particularly gratified by the exaltation of heart, and sudden sally of grateful feeling, with which the worthy Squire delivered one stanza: his eyes glistening, and his voice rambling out of all the bounds of time and tune:

> "'Tis Thou that crown'st my glittering hearth
>   With guiltlesse mirth,
> And giv'st me wassaile bowles to drink,
>   Spiced to the brink:
> Lord, 'tis Thy plenty-dropping hand
>   That soiles my land;
> And giv'st me for my bushell sowne,
>   Twice ten for one."

I afterwards understood that early morning service was read on every Sunday and saint's day throughout the year, either by Mr. Bracebridge or by some member of the family. It was once almost universally the case at the seats of the nobility and gentry of England, and it is much to be regretted that the custom is fallen into neglect; for the dullest observer must be sensible of the order and serenity prevalent in those households, where the occasional exercise of a beautiful form of worship in the morning gives, as it were, the key-note to every temper for the day, and attunes every spirit to harmony.

Our breakfast consisted of what the Squire denominated true old English fare. He indulged in some bitter lamentations over modern breakfasts of tea-and-toast, which he censured as among the causes of modern effeminacy and weak nerves, and

the decline of old English heartiness; and though he admitted them to his table to suit the palates of his guests, yet there was a brave display of cold meats, wine, and ale, on the sideboard.

After breakfast I walked about the grounds with Frank Bracebridge and Master Simon, or Mr. Simon, as he was called by everybody but the Squire. We were escorted by a number of gentleman-like dogs, that seemed loungers about the establishment; from the frisking spaniel to the steady old staghound; the last of which was of a race that had been in the family time out of mind: they were all obedient to a dog-whistle which hung to Master Simon's button-hole, and in the midst of

their gambols would glance an eye occasionally upon a small switch he carried in his hand.

The old mansion had a still more venerable look in the yellow sunshine than by pale moonlight; and I could not but feel the force of the Squire's idea, that the formal terraces, heavily moulded balustrades, and clipped yew-trees, carried with them an air of proud aristocracy. There appeared to be an unusual number of peacocks about the place, and I was making some remarks upon what I termed a flock of them, that were basking under a sunny wall, when I was gently corrected in my phraseology by Master Simon, who told me that, according to the most ancient and approved treatise on hunting, I must say a *muster* of peacocks. "In the same way," added he, with a slight air of pedantry, "we say a flight of doves or swallows, a bevy of quails, a herd of deer, of wrens, or cranes, a skulk of foxes, or a building of rooks." He went on to inform me, that according to Sir Anthony Fitzherbert, we ought to ascribe to this bird "both understanding and glory: for being praised, he will presently set up his tail chiefly against the sun, to the intent you may the better behold the beauty thereof. But at the fall of the leaf, when his tail falleth, he will mourn and hide himself in corners, till his tail come again as it was."

I could not help smiling at this display of small erudition on so whimsical a subject; but I found that the peacocks were birds of some consequence at the Hall, for Frank Bracebridge informed me that they were great favourites with his father, who was extremely careful to keep up the breed; partly because they belonged to chivalry, and were in great request at the stately banquets of the olden time; and partly because they had a pomp and magnificence about them, highly becoming an old family mansion. Nothing, he was accustomed to say, had an air of greater state and dignity than a peacock perched upon an antique stone balustrade.

Master Simon had now to hurry off, having an appointment at the parish church with the village choristers, who were to perform some music of his selection. There was something extremely agreeable in the cheerful flow of animal spirits of the little man; and I confess I had been somewhat surprised at his apt quotations from authors who certainly were not in the range of every-day reading. I mentioned this last circumstance to Frank Bracebridge, who told me with a smile that Master Simon's whole stock of erudition was confined to some half a dozen old authors, which the Squire had put into his hands, and which he read over and over, whenever he had a studious fit; as he sometimes had on a rainy day, or a long winter evening. Sir Anthony Fitzherbert's Book of Husbandry; Markham's Country Contentments; the Tretyse of Hunting, by Sir Thomas Cockayne, Knight; Izaak Walton's Angler, and two or three more such ancient worthies of the pen, were his standard authorities; and, like all men who know but a few

books, he looked up to them with a kind of idolatry, and quoted them on all occasions. As to his songs, they were chiefly picked out of old books in the Squire's library, and adapted to tunes that were popular among the choice spirits of the last century. His practical application of scraps of literature, however, had caused him to be looked upon as a prodigy of book-knowledge by all the grooms, huntsmen, and small sportsmen of the neighbourhood.

While we were talking we heard the distant toll of the village bell, and I was told that the Squire was a little particular in having his household at church on a Christmas morning; considering it a day of pouring out of thanks and rejoicing; for, as old Tusser observed,

> "At Christmas be merry, *and thankful withal*,
> And feast thy poor neighbours, the great and the small."

"If you are disposed to go to church," said Frank Bracebridge, "I can promise you a specimen of my cousin Simon's musical achievements. As the church is destitute of an organ, he has formed a band from the village amateurs, and established a musical club for their improvement; he has also sorted a choir, as he sorted my father's pack of hounds, according to the directions of Jervaise Markham, in his Country Contentments; for the bass he has sought out all the 'deep, solemn mouths,' and for the tenor the 'loud ringing mouths,' among the country bumpkins; and for 'sweet mouths,' he has culled with curious taste among the prettiest lasses in the neighbourhood: though these last, he affirms, are the most difficult to keep in tune; your pretty female singer being exceedingly wayward and capricious, and very liable to accident."

As the morning, though frosty, was remarkably fine and clear, the most of the family walked to the church, which was a very old building of gray stone, and stood near a village, about half a mile from the park gate. Adjoining it was a low snug parsonage, which seemed coeval with the church. The front of it was perfectly matted with a yew-tree that had been trained against its walls, through the dense foliage of which apertures had been formed to admit light into the small antique lattices. As we passed this sheltered nest, the parson issued forth and preceded us.

I had expected to see a sleek well-conditioned pastor, such as is often found in a snug living in the vicinity of a rich patron's table; but I was disappointed. The parson was a little, meagre, black-looking man, with a grizzled wig that was too wide, and stood off from each ear; so that his head seemed to have shrunk away within it, like a dried filbert in its shell. He wore a rusty coat, with great skirts, and pockets that would have held the church Bible and prayer-book; and his small legs seemed still smaller, from being planted in large shoes,

'On reaching the church-porch, we found the parson rebuking the gray-headed sexton for having used mistletoe.'

decorated with enormous buckles. I was informed by Frank Bracebridge that the parson had been a chum of his father's at Oxford, and had received this living shortly after the latter had come to his estate. He was a complete black-letter hunter, and would scarcely read a work printed in the Roman character. The editions of Caxton and Wynkin de Worde were his delight; and he was indefatigable in his researches after such old English writers as have fallen into oblivion from their worthlessness. In deference, perhaps, to the notions of Mr. Bracebridge, he had made diligent investigations into the festive rites and holiday customs of former times; and had been as zealous in the inquiry, as if he had been a boon companion; but it was merely with that plodding spirit with which men of adust temperament follow up any track of study, merely because it is denominated learning; indifferent to its intrinsic nature, whether it be the illustration of the wisdom, or of the ribaldry and obscenity of antiquity. He had pored over these old volumes so intensely, that they seemed to have been reflected into his countenance indeed; which, if the face be an index of the mind, might be compared to a title-page of black-letter.

On reaching the church-porch, we found the parson rebuking the gray-headed sexton for having used mistletoe among the greens with which the church was decorated. It was, he observed, an unholy plant, profaned by having been used by the Druids in their mystic ceremonies; and though it might be innocently employed in the festive ornamenting of halls and kitchens, yet it had been deemed by the Fathers of the Church as unhallowed, and totally unfit for sacred purposes. So tenacious was he on this point, that the poor sexton was obliged to strip down a great part of the humble trophies of his taste, before the parson would consent to enter upon the service of the day.

The interior of the church was venerable but simple; on

the walls were several mural monuments of the Bracebridges, and just beside the altar was a tomb of ancient workmanship, on

which lay the effigy of a warrior in armour, with his legs crossed, a sign of his having been a crusader. I was told it was one of the family who had signalised himself in the Holy Land, and the same whose picture hung over the fireplace in the hall. During service, Master Simon stood up in the pew, and repeated the responses very audibly; evincing that kind of ceremonious devotion punctually observed by a gentleman of the old school, and a man of old family connections. I observed, too, that he turned over the leaves of a folio prayer-book with something of a flourish; possibly to show off an enormous seal-ring which enriched one of his fingers, and which had the look of a family relic. But he was evidently most solicitous about the musical part of the service, keeping his eye

'The orchestra was in a small gallery, and presented a most whimsical grouping of heads.'

fixed intently on the choir, and beating time with much gesticulation and emphasis.

The orchestra was in a small gallery, and presented a most whimsical grouping of heads piled one above the other, among which I particularly noticed that of the village tailor, a pale fellow with a retreating forehead and chin, who played on the

clarionet, and seemed to have blown his face to a point; and there was another, a short pursy man, stooping and labouring at a bass viol, so as to show nothing but the top of a round bald head, like the egg of an ostrich. There were two or three pretty faces among the female singers, to which the keen air of a frosty morning had given a bright rosy tint; but the gentlemen choristers had evidently been chosen, like old Cremona fiddles, more for tone than looks; and as several had to sing from the same book, there were clusterings of odd physiognomies, not unlike those groups of cherubs we sometimes see on country tombstones.

The usual services of the choir were managed tolerably well, the vocal parts generally lagging a little behind the instrumental, and some loitering fiddler now and then making up for lost time by travelling over a passage with prodigious celerity, and clearing more bars than the keenest fox-hunter, to be in at the death. But the great trial was an anthem that had been prepared and arranged by Master Simon, and on which he had founded great expectation. Unluckily there

was a blunder at the very outset; the musicians became flurried; Master Simon was in a fever, everything went on lamely and irregularly until they came to a chorus beginning " Now let us sing with one accord," which seemed to be a signal for parting company ; all became discord and confusion ; each shifted for himself, and got to the end as well, or rather as soon, as he could, excepting one old chorister in a pair of horn spectacles bestriding and pinching a long sonorous nose; who, happening to stand a little apart, and being wrapped up in his own melody, kept on a quavering course, wriggling his head, ogling his book, and winding all up by a nasal solo of at least three bars' duration.

The parson gave us a most erudite sermon on the rites and ceremonies of Christmas, and the propriety of observing it not merely as a day of thanksgiving, but of rejoicing; supporting the correctness of his opinions by the earliest usages of the Church, and enforcing them by the authorities of Theophilus of Cesarea, St. Cyprian, St. Chrysostom, St. Augustine, and a cloud more of Saints and Fathers, from whom he made copious quotations. I was a little at a loss to perceive the necessity of such a mighty array of forces to maintain a point which no one present seemed inclined to dispute; but I soon found  that the good man had a legion of ideal adversaries to contend with; having, in the course of his researches on the subject of Christmas, got completely embroiled in the sectarian controversies of the Revolution, when the Puritans made such a fierce assault upon the ceremonies of the Church, and poor old Christmas was driven out of the land by proclamation of parliament.* The worthy parson lived but with times past, and knew but a little of the present.

* See Note C.

Shut up among worm-eaten tomes in the retirement of his antiquated little study, the pages of old times were to him as the gazettes of the day; while the era of the Revolution was mere modern history. He forgot that nearly two centuries had elapsed since the fiery persecution of poor mince-pie throughout the land; when plum-porridge was denounced as "mere popery," and roast beef as antichristian; and that Christmas had been brought in again triumphantly with the merry court of King Charles at the Restoration. He kindled into warmth with the ardour of his contest, and the host of imaginary foes with whom he had to combat; had a stubborn conflict with old Prynne and two or three other forgotten champions of the Roundheads, on the subject of Christmas festivity; and concluded by urging his hearers, in the most solemn and affecting manner, to stand to the traditionary customs of their fathers, and feast and make merry on this joyful anniversary of the Church.

I have seldom known a sermon attended apparently with more immediate effects; for on leaving the church the congregation seemed one and all possessed with the gaiety of spirit so earnestly enjoined by their pastor. The elder folks gathered in knots in the churchyard, greeting and shaking hands; and the children ran about crying, Ule! Ule! and repeating some uncouth rhymes,* which the parson, who had joined us, informed me had been handed down from days of yore. The villagers doffed their hats to the Squire as he passed, giving him the good wishes of the season with every appearance of heartfelt sincerity, and were invited by him to the hall, to take something to keep out the cold of the weather; and I heard blessings uttered by several of the poor, which convinced me that, in the midst of his enjoyments, the worthy old cavalier

---

* "Ule! Ule!
   Three puddings in a pule·
   Crack nuts and cry ule!"

had not forgotten the true Christmas virtue of charity. On our way homeward his heart seemed overflowing with generous and happy feelings. As we passed over a rising ground which commanded something of a prospect, the sounds of rustic merriment now and then reached our ears; the Squire paused for a few moments, and looked around with an air of inexpressible benignity. The beauty of the day was of

itself sufficient to inspire philanthropy. Notwithstanding the frostiness of the morning, the sun in his cloudless journey had acquired sufficient power to melt away the thin covering of snow from every southern declivity, and to bring out the living green which adorns an English landscape even in mid-winter. Large tracts of smiling verdure contrasted with the dazzling whiteness of the shaded slopes and hollows. Every sheltered bank, on which the broad rays rested, yielded its silver rill of cold and limpid water, glittering through the dripping grass;

and sent up slight exhalations to contribute to the thin haze that hung just above the surface of the earth. There was something truly cheering in this triumph of warmth and verdure over the frosty thraldom of winter; it was, as the Squire observed, an emblem of Christmas hospitality, breaking

through the chills of ceremony and selfishness, and thawing every heart into a flow.

He pointed with pleasure to the indications of good cheer reeking from the chimneys of the comfortable farm-houses and low thatched cottages. "I love," said he, "to see this day well kept by rich and poor; it is a great thing to have one day in the year, at least, when you are sure of being welcome wherever you go, and of having, as it were, the world all throw open to you; and I am almost disposed to join with Poor Robin, in his malediction of every churlish enemy to this honest festival :—

'Those who at Christmas do repine,
  And would fain hence despatch him,
May they with old Duke Humphry dine,
  Or else may Squire Ketch catch 'em.'"

The Squire went on to lament the deplorable decay of the games and amusements which were once prevalent at this season among the lower orders, and countenanced by the higher: when the old halls of castles and manor-houses were thrown open at daylight; when the tables were covered with brawn, and beef, and humming ale; when the harp and the carol resounded all day long, and when rich and poor were

alike welcome to enter and make merry." "Our old games and local customs," said he, "had a great effect in making the peasant fond of his home, and the promotion of them by the gentry made him fond of his lord. They made the times merrier, and kinder, and better; and I can truly say, with one of our old poets,—

'I like them well—the curious preciseness
  And all-pretended gravity of those
That seek to banish hence these harmless sports,
  Have thrust away much ancient honesty.'

* See Note D.

"The nation," continued he, "is altered; we have almost lost our simple true-hearted peasantry. They have broken asunder from the higher classes, and seem to think their interests are separate. They have become too knowing, and begin to read newspapers, listen to alehouse politicians, and talk of reform. I think one mode to keep them in good humour in these hard times would be for the nobility and gentry to pass more time on their estates, mingle more among the country people, and set the merry old English games going again."

Such was the good Squire's project for mitigating public discontent; and, indeed, he had once attempted to put his doctrine in practice, and a few years before had kept open house during the holidays in the old style. The country people, however, did not understand how to play their parts in the scene of hospitality; many uncouth circumstances occurred; the manor was overrun by all the vagrants of the country, and more beggars drawn into the neighbourhood in one week than the parish officers could get rid of in a year. Since then, he had contented himself with inviting the decent part of the neighbouring peasantry to call at the Hall on Christmas day, and distributing beef, and bread, and ale among the poor, that they might make merry in their own dwellings.

We had not been long home when the sound of music was heard from a distance. A band of country lads without coats, their shirt-sleeves fancifully tied with ribands, their hats decorated with greens, and clubs in their hands, were seen advancing up the avenue, followed by a large number of villagers and peasantry. They stopped before the hall door, where the music struck up a peculiar air, and the lads performed a curious and intricate dance, advancing, retreating, and striking their clubs together, keeping exact time to the music;

while one, whimsically crowned with a fox's skin, the tail of which flaunted down his back, kept capering round the skirts of the dance, and rattling a Christmas-box with many antic gesticulations.

The Squire eyed this fanciful exhibition with great interest and delight, and gave me a full account of its origin, which he traced to the times when the Romans held possession of the island; plainly proving that this was a lineal descendant of the sword-dance of the ancients. "It was now," he said, "nearly extinct, but he had accidentally met with traces of it in the neighbourhood, and had encouraged its revival; though, to tell the truth, it was too apt to be followed up by rough cudgel-play and broken heads in the evening."

After the dance was concluded, the whole party was

entertained with brawn and beef, and stout home-brewed. The Squire himself mingled among the rustics, and was received with awkward demonstrations of deference and regard. It is true I perceived two or three of the younger peasants, as they were raising their tankards to their mouths when the Squire's back was turned, making something of a grimace, and giving each other the wink; but the moment they caught my eye

they pulled grave faces, and were exceedingly demure. With Master Simon, however, they all seemed more at their ease. His varied occupations and amusements had made him well known throughout the neighbourhood. He was a visitor at every farm-house and cottage; gossiped with the farmers and their wives; romped with their daughters; and, like that type of a vagrant bachelor, the humble bee, tolled the sweets from all the rosy lips of the country round.

The bashfulness of the guests soon gave way before good cheer and affability. There is something genuine and affectionate in the gaiety of the lower orders, when it is excited by the bounty and familiarity of those above them; the warm glow of gratitude enters into their mirth, and a kind word or a small pleasantry, frankly uttered by a patron, gladdens the heart of the dependant more than oil and wine. When the Squire had retired the merriment increased, and there was much joking and laughter, particularly between Master Simon and a hale, ruddy-faced, white-headed farmer, who appeared to be the wit of the village; for I observed all his companions to wait with open mouths for his retorts, and burst into a gratuitous laugh before they could well understand them.  The whole house indeed seemed abandoned to merriment. As I passed to my room to dress for dinner, I heard the sound of music in a small court, and looking through a window that commanded it, I perceived a band of wandering musicians, with pandean pipes and tambourine; a pretty coquettish housemaid was dancing a jig with a smart country lad, while several of the other servants were looking on.  In the midst of her sport the girl caught a glimpse of my face at the window, and, colouring up, ran off with an air of roguish affected confusion.

The Christmas Dinner

Lo, now is come the joyful'st feast!
　Let every man be jolly,
Eache roome with yvie leaves is drest,
　And every post with holly.
Now all our neighbours' chimneys smoke,
　And Christmas blocks are burning;
Their ovens they with bak't meats choke,
　And all their spits are turning.
　　Without the door let sorrow lie,
　　　And if, for cold, it hap to die,
　　We'll bury't in a Christmas pye,
　　　And evermore be merry.
　　　　　　　WITHERS'S *Juvenilia*.

THE CHRISTMAS DINNER

I HAD finished my toilet, and was loitering with Frank Bracebridge in the library, when we heard a distant thwacking sound, which he informed me was a signal for the serving up of the dinner. The Squire kept up old customs in kitchen as well as hall; and the rolling-pin, struck upon the dresser by the cook, summoned the servants to carry in the meats.

> Just in this nick the cook knock'd thrice,
> And all the waiters in a trice
>   His summons did obey;
> Each serving man, with dish in hand,
> March'd boldly up, like our train-band,
>   Presented and away.*

* Sir John Suckling.

The dinner was served up in the great hall, where the Squire always held his Christmas banquet. A blazing crackling fire of logs had been heaped on to warm the spacious apartment, and the flame went sparkling and wreathing up the wide-mouthed chimney. The great picture of the crusader and his white horse had

been profusely decorated with greens for the occasion; and holly and ivy had likewise been wreathed round the helmet and weapons on the opposite wall, which I understood were the arms of the same warrior. I must own, by the bye, I had strong doubts about the authenticity of the painting and armour as having belonged to the crusader, they certainly having the stamp of more recent days; but I was told that the painting had been so considered time out of mind; and that as to the armour, it had been found in a lumber room, and elevated to its present situation by the Squire, who at once determined it to be the armour of the family hero; and as he was absolute authority on all such

'Never did Christmas board display a more goodly and gracious assemblage of countenances.'

subjects in his own household, the matter had passed into current acceptation. A sideboard was set out just under this chivalric trophy, on which was a display of plate that might have vied (at least in variety) with Belshazzar's parade of the vessels of the temple; "flagons, cans, cups, beakers, goblets,

basins, and ewers;" the gorgeous utensils of good companionship, that had gradually accumulated through many generations of jovial housekeepers. Before these stood the two Yule candles beaming like two stars of the first magnitude; other lights were distributed in branches, and the whole array glittered like a firmament of silver.

We were ushered into this banqueting scene with the sound of minstrelsy, the old harper being seated on a stool beside the fireplace, and twanging his instrument with a vast deal more power than melody. Never did Christmas board display a more goodly and gracious assemblage of countenances: those who were not handsome were, at least, happy; and happiness is a rare improver of your hard-favoured visage. I always consider an old English family as well worth studying as a collection of Holbein's portraits or Albert Dürer's prints.

There is much antiquarian lore to be acquired ; much knowledge of the physiognomies of former times. Perhaps it may be from  having continually before their eyes those rows of old family portraits, with which the mansions of this country are stocked ; certain it is, that the quaint features of antiquity are often most faithfully perpetuated in these ancient lines ; and I have traced an old family nose through a whole picture gallery, legitimately handed down from generation to generation, almost from the time of the Conquest. Something of the kind was to be observed in the worthy company around me. Many of their faces had evidently originated in a Gothic age, and been merely copied by succeeding generations ; and there was one little girl, in particular, of staid demeanour, with a high Roman nose, and an antique vinegar aspect, who was a great favourite of the Squire's, being, as he said, a Bracebridge all over, and the very counterpart of one of his ancestors who figured in the court of Henry VIII.

The parson said grace, which was not a short familiar one, such as is commonly addressed to the Deity, in these unceremonious days ; but a long, courtly, well-worded one of the ancient school. There was now a pause, as if something was expected; when suddenly the butler entered the hall with some degree of bustle; he was attended by a servant on each side with a large wax-light, and bore a silver dish, on which was an enormous pig's head decorated with rosemary, with a lemon

in its mouth, which was placed with great formality at the head of the table. The moment this pageant made its appearance, the harper struck up a flourish; at the conclusion of which the young Oxonian, on receiving a hint from the Squire, gave, with an air of the most comic gravity, an old carol, the first verse of which was as follows:—

> " Caput apri defero
> Reddens laudes Domino.

> The boar's head in hand bring I,
> With garlands gay and rosemary.
> I pray you all synge merily
> Qui estis in convivio."

Though prepared to witness many of these little eccentricities, from being apprised of the peculiar hobby of mine host; yet, I confess, the parade with which so odd a dish was introduced somewhat perplexed me, until I gathered from the conversation of the Squire and the parson that it was meant to represent the bringing in of the boar's head: a dish formerly served up with much ceremony, and the sound of minstrelsy and song, at great tables on Christmas day. "I like the old custom," said the Squire, "not merely because it is stately and pleasing in itself, but because it was observed at the College of Oxford, at which I was educated. When I hear the old song chanted, it brings to mind the time when I was young and gamesome—and the noble old college-hall—and my fellow students loitering about in their black gowns; many of whom, poor lads, are now in their graves!"

The parson, however, whose mind was not haunted by such associations, and who was always more taken up with the text than the sentiment, objected to the Oxonian's version of the carol: which he affirmed was different from that sung at college. He went on, with the dry perseverance of a commentator, to give the college reading, accompanied by sundry annotations: addressing himself at first to the company at large; but finding their attention gradually diverted to other talk, and other objects, he lowered his tone as his number of auditors diminished, until he concluded his remarks, in an under voice, to a fat-headed old gentleman next him, who was silently engaged in the discussion of a huge plateful of turkey.*

The table was literally loaded with good cheer, and presented an epitome of country abundance, in this season of overflowing

---

* See Note E.

larders. A distinguished post was allotted to "ancient sirloin," as mine host termed it; being, as he added, "the standard of

old English hospitality, and a joint of goodly presence, and full of expectation." There were several dishes quaintly decorated, and which had evidently something traditionary in their embellishments; but about which, as I did not like to appear over-curious, I asked no questions.

I could not, however, but notice a pie, magnificently decorated with peacocks' feathers, in imitation of the tail of that bird, which overshadowed a considerable tract of the table. This the Squire confessed, with some little hesitation, was a pheasant-pie, though a peacock-pie was certainly the most authentical; but there had been such a mortality among the peacocks this season, that he could not prevail upon himself to have one killed.*

It would be tedious, perhaps, to my wiser readers, who may not have that foolish fondness for odd and obsolete things to which I am a little given, were I to mention the other make-shifts of this worthy old humorist, by which he was endeavouring to follow up, though at humble distance, the quaint customs of antiquity. I was pleased, however, to see the respect shown to his whims by his children and relatives; who, indeed, entered readily into the full spirit of them, and seemed all well versed in their parts; having doubtless been present at many a rehearsal. I was amused, too, at the air of profound gravity with which the butler and other servants executed the duties assigned them, however eccentric. They had an old-fashioned look; having, for the most part, been brought up in the household, and grown into keeping with the antiquated mansion, and the humours of its lord; and most probably looked upon all his whimsical regulations as the established laws of honourable housekeeping.

When the cloth was removed, the butler brought in a huge silver vessel of rare and curious workmanship, which he placed before the Squire. Its appearance was hailed with acclamation; being the Wassail Bowl, so renowned in Christmas festivity. The contents had been prepared by the Squire himself; for it was a beverage in the skilful mixture of which he particularly prided himself; alleging that it was too abstruse and complex for the comprehension of an ordinary servant. It was a potation, indeed, that might well make the heart of a toper leap within him; being composed of the richest and raciest

* See Note F.

wines, highly spiced and sweetened, with roasted apples bobbing about the surface.*

The old gentleman's whole countenance beamed with a serene look of indwelling delight, as he stirred this mighty

bowl. Having raised it to his lips, with a hearty wish of a merry Christmas to all present, he sent it brimming round the board, for every one to follow his example, according to the primitive style; pronouncing it "the ancient fountain of good feeling, where all hearts met together."†

There was much laughing and rallying as the honest emblem of Christmas joviality circulated, and was kissed rather coyly by the ladies. When it reached Master Simon he raised it in both hands, and with the air of a boon companion struck up an old Wassail chanson:

> The browne bowle,
> The merry browne bowle,

* See Note G.   † See Note H.

As it goes round about-a,
    Fill
    Still,
Let the world say what it will,
And drink your fill all out-a.

The deep canne,
The merry deep canne,
As thou dost freely quaff-a,
    Sing,
    Fling,
Be as merry as a king,
And sound a lusty laugh-a.*

    Much of the conversation during dinner turned upon family topics, to which I was a stranger. There was, however, a great deal of rallying of Master Simon about some gay widow, with

* From "Poor Robin's Almanack."

whom he was accused of having a flirtation. This attack was commenced by the ladies; but it was continued throughout the dinner by the fat-headed old gentleman next the parson, with the persevering assiduity of a slow-hound; being one of those long-winded jokers, who, though rather dull at starting game, are unrivalled for their talents in hunting it down. At every pause in the general conversation, he renewed his bantering in pretty much the same terms; winking hard at me with both eyes whenever he gave Master Simon what he considered a home thrust.  The latter, indeed, seemed fond of being teased on the subject, as old bachelors are apt to be; and he took occasion to inform me, in an under-tone, that the lady in question was a prodigiously fine woman, and drove her own curricle.

The dinner-time passed away in this flow of innocent hilarity; and, though the old hall may have resounded in its time with many a scene of broader rout and revel, yet I doubt whether it ever witnessed more honest and genuine enjoyment. How easy it is for one benevolent being to diffuse pleasure around him; and how truly is a kind heart a fountain of gladness, making everything in its vicinity to freshen into smiles! the joyous disposition of the worthy Squire was perfectly contagious; he was happy himself, and disposed to make all the world happy; and the little eccentricities of his humour did but season, in a manner, the sweetness of his philanthropy.

When the ladies had retired, the conversation, as usual, became still more animated; many good things were broached which had been thought of during dinner, but which would not exactly do for a lady's ear; and though I cannot positively

affirm that there was much wit uttered, yet I have certainly heard many contests of rare wit produce much less laughter. Wit, after all, is a mighty tart, pungent ingredient, and much too acid for some stomachs; but honest good-humour is the oil and wine of a merry meeting, and there is no jovial companionship equal to that where the jokes are rather small, and the laughter abundant. The Squire told several long stories of early college pranks and adventures, in some of which the parson had been a sharer; though in looking at the latter, it required some effort of imagination to figure such a little dark anatomy of a man into the perpetrator of a madcap gambol. Indeed, the two college chums presented pictures of what men may be made by their different lots in life. The Squire had left the university to live lustily on his paternal domains, in the vigorous enjoyment

of prosperity and sunshine, and had flourished on to a hearty and florid old age; whilst the poor parson, on the contrary, had dried and withered away, among dusty tomes, in the silence and shadows of his study. Still there seemed to be a spark of almost extinguished fire, feebly glimmering in the bottom of his soul; and as the Squire hinted at a sly story of the parson and a pretty milkmaid, whom they once met on the banks of the Isis, the old gentleman made an "alphabet of faces," which, as far as I could decipher his physiognomy, I verily believe was indicative of laughter;—indeed, I have rarely met with an old gentleman who took absolutely offence at the imputed gallantries of his youth.

I found the tide of wine and wassail fast gaining on the dry land of sober judgment. The company grew merrier and louder as their jokes grew duller. Master Simon was in as

chirping a humour as a grasshopper filled with dew; his old songs grew of a warmer complexion, and he began to talk maudlin about the widow. He even gave a long song about the wooing of a widow, which he informed me he had gathered from an excellent black-letter work, entitled "Cupid's Solicitor for Love," containing store of good advice for bachelors, and which he promised to lend me. The first verse was to this effect:—

> He that will woo a widow must not dally,
> He must make hay while the sun doth shine;
> He must not stand with her, Shall I, Shall I?
> But boldly say, Widow, thou must be mine.

This song inspired the fat-headed old gentleman, who made several attempts to tell a rather broad story out of Joe Miller, that was pat to the purpose; but he always stuck in the middle, everybody recollecting the latter part excepting himself. The parson, too, began to show the effects of good cheer, having gradually settled down into a doze, and his wig sitting most suspiciously on one side. Just at this juncture we were summoned to the drawing-room, and, I suspect, at the private instigation of mine host, whose joviality seemed always tempered with a proper love of decorum.

After the dinner-table was removed, the hall was given up to the younger members of the family, who, prompted to all kind of noisy mirth by the Oxonian and Master Simon, made its old walls ring with their merriment, as they played at romping games. I delight in witnessing the gambols of children, and particularly at this happy holiday-season, and could not help stealing out of the drawing-room on hearing one of their peals of laughter. I found them at the game of blind-man's buff. Master Simon, who was the leader of their revels, and seemed on all occasions to fulfil the office of that ancient potentate, the Lord of Misrule,* was blinded in the midst of the hall. The little beings were as busy about him as the mock fairies about Falstaff; pinching him, plucking at the skirts of his coat, and tickling him with straws. One fine blue-eyed girl of about thirteen, with her flaxen hair all in beautiful confusion, her frolic face in a glow, her frock half torn off her shoulders, a complete picture of a romp, was the chief tormentor; and from the slyness with which Master Simon avoided the smaller game, and hemmed this wild little nymph in corners, and obliged her to jump shrieking over chairs, I suspected the rogue of being not a whit more blinded than was convenient.

When I returned to the drawing-room, I found the company

* See Note I.

seated round the fire, listening to the parson, who was deeply ensconced in a high-backed oaken chair, the work of some cunning artificer of yore, which had been brought from the library for his particular accommodation. From this venerable piece of furniture, with which his shadowy figure and dark weazen face so admirably accorded, he was dealing forth strange accounts of the popular superstitions and legends of the surrounding country, with which he had become acquainted in the course of his antiquarian researches. I am half inclined to think that the old gentleman was himself somewhat tinctured with superstition, as men are very apt to be who live a recluse and studious life in a sequestered part of the country, and pore over black-letter tracts, so often filled with the marvellous and supernatural.

He gave us several anecdotes of the fancies of the neigh-

bouring peasantry, concerning the effigy of the crusader which lay on the tomb by the church altar. As it was the only monument of the kind in that part of the country, it had always been regarded with feelings of superstition by the goodwives of the village. It was said to get up from the tomb and walk the rounds of the churchyard in stormy nights, particularly when it thundered; and one old woman, whose cottage bordered on the churchyard, had seen it, through the windows of the church, when the moon shone, slowly pacing up and down the aisles. It was the belief that some wrong had been left unredressed by the deceased, or some treasure hidden, which kept the spirit in a state of trouble and restlessness. Some talked of gold and jewels buried in the tomb, over which the spectre kept watch; and there was a story current of a sexton in old times who endeavoured to break his way to the coffin at night; but just as he reached it, received a violent blow from the marble hand of the effigy, which stretched him senseless on the pavement. These tales were often laughed at by some of the sturdier among the rustics, yet when night came on, there were many of the stoutest unbelievers that were shy of venturing alone in the footpath that led across the churchyard.

From these and other anecdotes that followed, the crusader appeared to be the favourite hero of ghost stories throughout the vicinity. His picture, which hung up in the hall, was

thought by the servants to have something supernatural about it; for they remarked that, in whatever part of the hall you went, the eyes of the warrior were still fixed on you. The old porter's wife, too, at the lodge, who had been born and brought up in the family, and was a great gossip among the maid-servants, affirmed, that in her young days she had often heard say, that on Midsummer eve, when it is well known all kinds of ghosts, goblins, and fairies become visible and walk abroad, the crusader used to mount his horse, come down from his picture, ride about the house, down the avenue, and so to

the church to visit the tomb; on which occasion the church-door most civilly swung open of itself: not that he needed it; for he rode through closed gates and even stone walls, and had been seen by one of the dairymaids to pass between two bars of the great park gate, making himself as thin as a sheet of paper.

All these superstitions I found had been very much countenanced by the Squire, who, though not superstitious himself, was very fond of seeing others so. He listened to every goblin tale of the neighbouring gossips with infinite gravity, and held the porter's wife in high favour on account of her talent for the marvellous. He was himself a great reader of old legends and romances, and often lamented that he could not believe in them; for a superstitious person, he thought, must live in a kind of fairyland.

Whilst we were all attention to the parson's stories, our ears were suddenly assailed by a burst of heterogeneous sounds from the hall, in which was mingled something like the clang of rude minstrelsy, with the uproar of many small voices and girlish laughter. The door suddenly flew open, and a train came trooping into the room, that might almost have been mistaken for the breaking up of the court of Fairy. That indefatigable spirit, Master Simon, in the faithful discharge of his duties as Lord of Misrule, had conceived the idea of a Christmas mummery, or masking; and having called in to his assistance the Oxonion and the young officer, who were equally ripe for anything that should occasion romping and merriment, they had carried it into instant effect. The old housekeeper had been consulted; the antique clothes-presses and wardrobes rummaged and made to yield up the relics of finery that had not seen the light for several generations; the younger part of the company had been privately convened from the parlour and hall, and the whole had been bedizened out, into a burlesque imitation of an antique masque.*

Master Simon led the van, as "Ancient Christmas," quaintly apparelled in a ruff, a short cloak, which had very much the aspect of one of the old housekeeper's petticoats, and a hat that might have served for a village steeple, and must indubitably have figured in the days of the Covenanters. From under this his nose curved boldly forth, flushed with a frost-bitten bloom, that seemed the very trophy of a December blast. He was accompanied by the blue-eyed romp, dished up as "Dame Mince-Pie," in the venerable magnificence of faded brocade, long stomacher, peaked hat, and high-heeled shoes. The young officer appeared as Robin Hood, in a sporting dress of Kendal green, and a foraging cap, with a gold tassel. The

* See Note J.

costume, to be sure, did not bear testimony to deep research, and there was an evident eye to the picturesque, natural to a young gallant in the presence of his mistress. The fair Julia hung on his arm in a pretty rustic dress, as "Maid Marian."

The rest of the train had been metamorphosed in various ways; the girls trussed up in the finery of the ancient belles of the Bracebridge line, and the striplings bewhiskered with burnt cork, and gravely clad in broad skirts, hanging sleeves, and full-bottomed wigs, to represent the characters of Roast Beef, Plum

'The rest of the train had been metamorphosed in various ways.'

Pudding, and other worthies celebrated in ancient maskings. The whole was under the control of the Oxonian, in the appropriate character of Misrule; and I observed that he exercised rather a mischievous sway with his wand over the smaller personages of the pageant.

The irruption of this motley crew, with beat of drum, according to ancient custom, was the consummation of uproar and merriment. Master Simon covered himself with glory by the stateliness with which, as Ancient Christmas, he walked a minuet with the peerless, though giggling, Dame Mince-Pie. It was followed by a dance of all the characters, which, from its medley of costumes, seemed as though the old family portraits had skipped down from their frames to join in the sport. Different centuries were figuring at cross hands and right and left; the dark ages were cutting pirouettes and rigadoons; and the days of Queen Bess jigging merrily down the middle, through a line of succeeding generations.

The worthy squire contemplated these fantastic sports, and this resurrection of his old wardrobe, with the simple relish of childish delight. He stood chuckling and rubbing his hands, and scarcely hearing a word the parson said, notwithstanding that the latter was discoursing most authentically on the ancient and stately dance at the Paon, or Peacock, from which he conceived the minuet to be derived.*

For my part, I was in a continual excitement, from the varied scenes of whim and innocent gaiety passing before

me. It was inspiring to see wild-eyed frolic and warm-hearted hospitality breaking out from among the chills and glooms of winter, and old age throwing off his apathy, and catching once more the freshness of youthful enjoyment. I

* See Note K.

felt also an interest in the scene, from the consideration that these fleeting customs were posting fast into oblivion, and that this was, perhaps, the only family in England in which the whole of them were still punctiliously observed. There was a quaintness, too, mingled with all this revelry that gave it a peculiar zest; it was suited to the time and place;

and as the old Manor House almost reeled with mirth and wassail, it seemed echoing back the joviality of long-departed years.

But enough of Christmas and its gambols; it is time for me to pause in this garrulity. Methinks I hear the questions asked by my graver readers, "To what purpose is all this?—how is the world to be made wiser by this talk?" Alas! is there not wisdom enough extant for the instruction of the world?

And if not, are there not thousands of abler pens labouring for its improvement?—It is so much pleasanter to please than to instruct—to play the companion rather than the preceptor.

What, after all, is the mite of wisdom that I could throw into the mass of knowledge? or how am I sure that my sagest deductions may be safe guides for the opinions of others. But in writing to amuse, if I fail, the only evil is my own disappointment. If, however, I can by any lucky chance, in these days of evil, rub out one wrinkle from the brow of care, or beguile the heavy heart of one moment of sorrow; if I can now and then penetrate through the gathering film of misanthropy, prompt a benevolent view of human nature, and make my reader more in good-humour with his fellow beings and himself, surely, surely, I shall not then have written entirely in vain.

NOTES

NOTE A, p. 38.

THE mistletoe is still hung up in farm-houses and kitchens at Christmas: and the young men have the privilege of kissing the girls under it, plucking each time a berry from the bush. When the berries are all plucked, the privilege ceases.

NOTE B, pp. 43, 53.

The *Yule-clog* is a great log of wood, sometimes the root of a tree, brought into the house with great ceremony, on Christmas eve, laid in the fireplace, and lighted with the brand of last year's clog. While it lasted there was great drinking, singing, and telling of tales. Sometimes it was accompanied by Christmas candles, but in the cottages the only light was from the ruddy blaze of the great wood fire. The *Yule-clog* was to burn all night; if it went out, it was considered a sign of ill luck.

Herrick mentions it in one of his songs:

> "Come, bring with a noise
> My merrie, merrie boyes,
> The Christmas log to the firing:
> While my good dame, she
> Bids ye all be free,
> And drink to your hearts' desiring."

The *Yule-clog* is still burnt in many farm-houses and kitchens in England, particularly in the north, and there are several superstitions connected with it among the peasantry. If a squinting person come to the house while it is burning, or a person barefooted, it is considered an ill omen. The brand remaining from the *Yule-clog* is carefully put away to light the next year's Christmas fire.

Note C, p. 75.

From the "Flying Eagle," a small Gazette, published December 24, 1652:—"The House spent much time this day about the business of the Navy, for settling the affairs at sea; and before they rose, were presented with a terrible remonstrance against Christmas day, grounded upon divine Scriptures, 2 Cor. v. 16; 1 Cor. xv. 14, 17; and in honour of the Lord's Day, grounded upon these Scriptures, John xx. 1; Rev. i. 10; Psalm cxviii. 24; Lev. xxiii. 7, 11; Mark xvi. 8; Psalm lxxxiv. 10, in which Christmas is called Anti-Christ's masse, and those Mass-mongers and Papists who observe it, etc. In consequence of which Parliament spent some time in consultation about the abolition of Christmas day, passed orders to that effect, and resolved to sit on the following day, which was commonly called Christmas day."

Note D, p. 79.

"An English gentleman at the opening of the great day, *i.e.* on Christmas day in the morning, had all his tenants and neighbours enter his hall by daybreak. The strong beer was broached, and the black jacks went plentifully about with toast, sugar, nutmeg, and good Cheshire cheese. The hackin (the great sausage) must be boiled by daybreak, or else two young men must take the maiden (*i.e.* the cook) by the arms and run her round the market-place till she is shamed of her laziness."—*Round about our Sea-Coal Fire.*

Note E, p. 94.

The old ceremony of serving up the boar's head on Christmas day is still observed in the hall of Queen's College, Oxford. I was favoured by the parson with a copy of the carol as now sung, and as it may be acceptable to such of my readers as are curious in these grave and learned matters, I give it entire.

> "The boar's head in hand bear I,
> Bedeck'd with bays and rosemary;
> And I pray you, my masters, be merry
> Quot estis in convivio.
>   Caput apri defero
>   Reddens laudes Domino.

> The boar's head, as I understand,
> Is the rarest dish in all this land,
> Which thus bedeck'd with a gay garland
>   Let us servire cantico.
>   Caput apri defero, etc.
>
> Our Steward hath provided this
> In honour of the King of Bliss,
> Which on this day to be served is
>   In Reginensi Atrio.
>   Caput apri defero,"
>   Etc. etc. etc.

Note F. p. 96.

The peacock was anciently in great demand for stately entertainments. Sometimes it was made into a pie, at one end of which the head appeared above the crust in all its plumage, with the beak richly gilt; at the other end the tail was displayed. Such pies were served up at the solemn banquets of chivalry, when Knights-errant pledged themselves to undertake any perilous enterprise; whence came the ancient oath, used by Justice Shallow, " by cock and pie."

The peacock was also an important dish for the Christmas feast; and Massinger, in his City Madam, gives some idea of the extravagance with which this, as well as other dishes, was prepared for the gorgeous revels of the olden times:—

> " Men may talk of country Christmasses,
>   Their thirty pound butter'd eggs, their pies of carps' tongues:
>   Their pheasants drench'd with ambergris: *the carcases of three fat wethers bruised for gravy, to make sauce for a single peacock!*"

Note G. p. 97.

The Wassail Bowl was sometimes composed of ale instead of wine: with nutmeg, sugar, toast, ginger, and roasted crabs; in this way the nut-brown beverage is still prepared in some old families, and round the hearths of substantial farmers at Christmas. It is also called Lambs' Wool, and is celebrated by Herrick in his " Twelfth Night:"—

> " Next crowne the bowle full
>   With gentle Lambs' Wool,

> Add sugar, nutmeg, and ginger,
> With store of ale too:
> And thus ye must doe
> To make the Wassaile a swinger."

Note H, p. 97.

"The custom of drinking out of the same cup gave place to each having his cup. When the steward came to the doore with the Wassel, he was to cry three times, *Wassel, Wassel, Wassel*, and then the chappel (chaplain) was to answer with a song.—ARCHÆOLOGIA.

Note I, p. 102.

"At Christmasse there was in the Kinge's house, wheresoever hee was lodged, a lorde of misrule, or mayster of merry disportes; and the like had ye in the house of every nobleman of honor, or good worshippe, were he spirituall or temporall."—STOW.

Note J, p. 107.

Maskings or mummeries were favourite sports at Christmas in old times: and the wardrobes at halls and manor-houses were often laid under contribution to furnish dresses and fantastic disguisings. I strongly suspect Master Simon to have taken the idea of his from Ben Jonson's Masque of Christmas.

Note K, p. 112.

Sir John Hawkins, speaking of the dance called the Pavon, from *pavo*, a peacock, says, "It is a grave and majestic dance; the method of dancing it anciently was by gentlemen dressed with caps and swords, by those of the long robe in their gowns, by the peers in their mantles, and by the ladies in gowns with long trains, the motion whereof, in dancing, resembled that of a peacock." –*History of Music*.

BRACEBRIDGE HALL

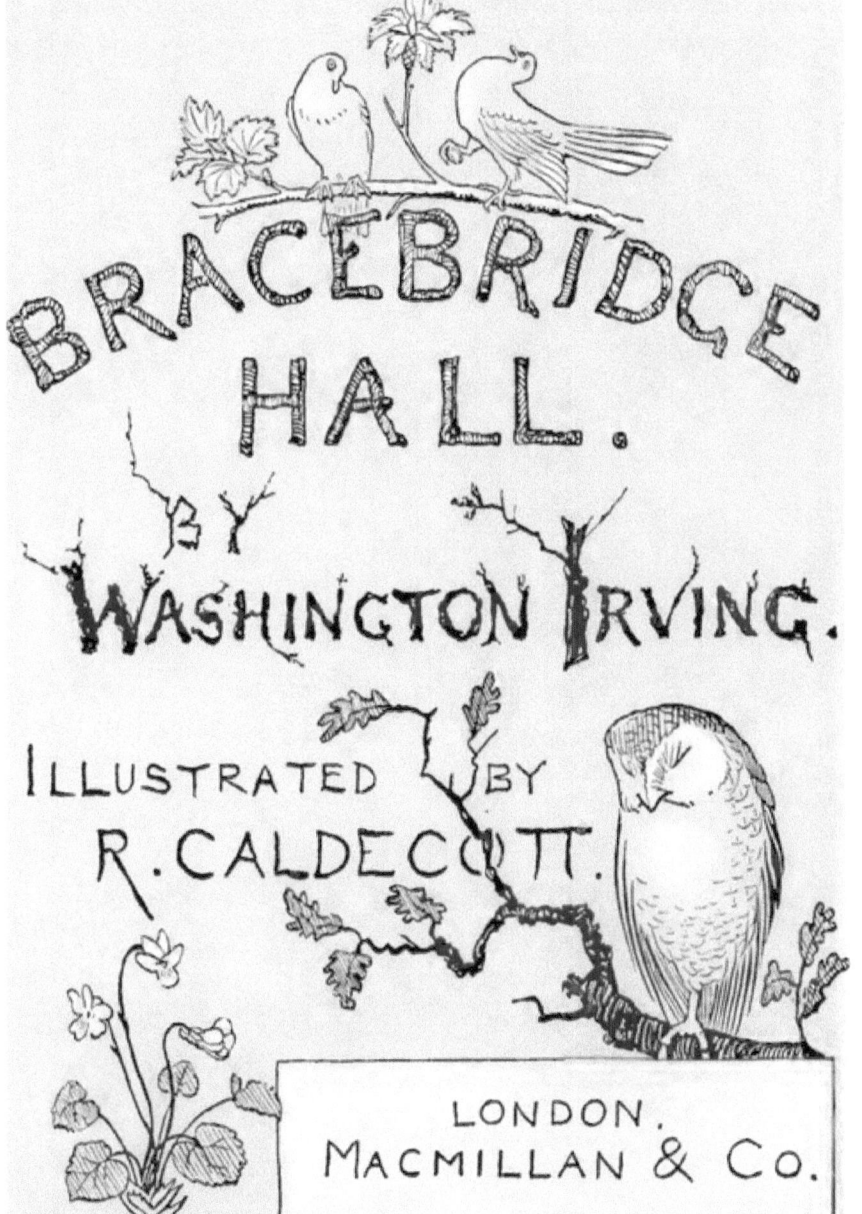

The success of "OLD CHRISTMAS" has suggested the re-publication of its sequel "BRACEBRIDGE HALL," illustrated by the same able pencil, but condensed so as to bring it within reasonable size and price.

	PAGE
THE HALL	135
THE BUSY MAN	140
FAMILY SERVANTS	147
THE WIDOW	156
THE LOVERS	162
FAMILY RELIQUES	168
AN OLD SOLDIER	175
THE WIDOW'S RETINUE	180
READY-MONEY JACK	185
BACHELORS	192
A LITERARY ANTIQUARY	199
THE FARM-HOUSE	206
HORSEMANSHIP	211
LOVE SYMPTOMS	217
FALCONRY	221
HAWKING	227
FORTUNE-TELLING	235
LOVE-CHARMS	241
A BACHELOR'S CONFESSIONS	247

CONTENTS

	PAGE
GIPSIES	254
VILLAGE WORTHIES .	260
THE SCHOOLMASTER .	264
THE SCHOOL .	272
A VILLAGE POLITICIAN	277
THE ROOKERY	283
MAY-DAY	292
THE CULPRIT	306
LOVERS' TROUBLES .	317
THE WEDDING	324

DESIGNED BY RANDOLPH CALDECOTT,

AND

ARRANGED AND ENGRAVED BY J. D. COOPER.

	PAGE
TITLE-PAGE	
HEADING TO PREFACE	123
TAILPIECE TO PREFACE	123
HEADING TO CONTENTS	125
TAILPIECE TO CONTENTS	126
HEADING TO LIST OF ILLUSTRATIONS	127
TAILPIECE TO ILLUSTRATIONS	132
THE HAWKING PARTY	134
THE HALL	135
THE TERRACE GARDEN	137
STOPPING TO GATHER A FLOWER	138
BREAKING A POINTER	140
THE CHILDREN DANCE IN THE HALL	142
"SEVERAL UNHAPPY BIRDS IN DURANCE"	143

LIST OF ILLUSTRATIONS

	PAGE
OLD CHRISTY	144
"TWO PAMPERED CURS THAT BARKED OUT OF EACH WINDOW"	145
ARRIVAL OF THE WIDOW	146
HEADING TO "FAMILY SERVANTS"	147
THE OLD HOUSEKEEPER	148
PHŒBE WILKINS	150
"SHE DRINKS THE HEALTH OF THE COMPANY"	151
CONTEMPLATION	154
THE WIDOW	156
KENSINGTON GARDENS	158
A SAGE ADVISER	160
MASTER SIMON OVER THE ACCOUNTS	161
HEADING TO "THE LOVERS"	162
THE LOVERS	164
THE TRIO	167
HEADING TO "FAMILY RELIQUES"	168
EFFIGY IN MARBLE	171
JULIA AND THE CAPTAIN IN THE GALLERY	173
THE SALUTATION	175
GENERAL HARBOTTLE	177
"PUBLIC DISTRESS, SIR, IS ALL HUMBUG!"	179
CANINE PETS	180
THE OLD COACHMAN	181
DIGNITY AND IMPUDENCE	183
CONFIDENTIAL WHISPER	184
READY-MONEY JACK EXPOUNDING	185
IN AT THE DEATH	188

LIST OF ILLUSTRATIONS

	PAGE
Quelling the Brawl	189
Quarter-Staff	191
Mulligatawney Club	192
Chaffing the Milkmaid	195
Conjugal Extinguisher	197
A Literary Antiquary	199
A Bookworm	202
"Come, tell me, says Rosa, as kissing and kissed"	204
Heading to "The Farm-House"	206
"He shone like a Bottle"	208
A Tailpiece	210
Christy on Pepper	211
A Hunter	214
The Tutor's Dismissal	215
The Offering	217
Mrs. Hannah	219
Asleep when he reads	220
Falconry in Olden Times	221
Physicking the Hawks	224
"Well, well, have it your own way, Christy!"	225
Hawking	227
The Consultation in the Field	229
The Quarry in sight	231
Julia's Mishap	232
Pluming her Wings	234
The Gipsy Encampment	235
A Gipsy Girl	236
The General in the Toils	237

LIST OF ILLUSTRATIONS

	PAGE
"God save the King!"	240
Tossing the Pancake	241
Jack jilts Phœbe	244
The Love-Spell	245
Master Simon at the Window	247
Master Simon in Love	249
Gentlemen's Jokes	253
Starlight Tom on the Watch	254
A Gipsy Party	256
Fortune-telling	259
Heading to "Village Worthies"	260
"Master Simon pinched the Daughter's Cheek"	261
The Apothecary	263
Heading to "The Schoolmaster"	264
Slingsby and Ready-Money Jack	267
"On the Road"	270
The School	272
The Prodigal	274
The Truants	275
Laying down the Law	277
The Village Politician	279
The Landlady	280
The Antagonists	282
The Rookery	283
After the Straws	285
Rooks on the Sheep	287
The Hermit Owl	289
Bachelor's Hall	291

		PAGE
May-Day		292
May-Day Queen		294
The General nonplussed		297
May Queen and Bride-Elect		298
May-Day Melée		301
Rumpled Feathers		304
The Capture		306
Conscience makes Cowards of the Dogs		307
The Tribunal		309
The Guard		313
Tailpiece		316
A Solemn Consultation		317
Love Documents		320
Slingsby and Phœbe		322
Butler with Bride Cup		324
The Wedding		327
Rural Artillery		329
Master Simon opens the Ball		330
Reconciliation		333
A Maiden Confession		334
Master Simon's Finale		337

'The chivalry of the Hall prepared to take the field.'—PAGE 228.

THE HALL

The ancientest house, and the best for housekeeping in this county or the next, and though the master of it write but squire, I know no lord like him.

Merry Beggars.

THE reader, if he has perused the volumes of the Sketch Book, will probably recollect something of the Bracebridge family, with which I once passed a Christmas. I am now on another visit at the Hall, having been invited to a wedding which is shortly to take place. The Squire's second son, Guy, a fine, spirited young captain in the army, is about to be married to his father's ward, the fair Julia Templeton. A gathering of relations and friends has already commenced, to celebrate the joyful occasion; for the old gentleman is an enemy to quiet, private weddings. "There is nothing," he says, "like launching a young couple gaily, and cheering them from the shore; a good outset is half the voyage."

Before proceeding any farther, I would beg that the Squire might not be confounded with that class of hard-riding, fox-hunting gentlemen so often described, and, in fact, so nearly extinct in England. I use this rural title, partly because it is his universal appellation throughout the neighbourhood, and partly because it saves me the frequent repetition of his name, which is one of those rough old English names at which Frenchmen exclaim in despair.

The Squire is, in fact, a lingering specimen of the old English country gentleman; rusticated a little by living almost entirely on his estate, and something of a humorist, as Englishmen are apt to become when they have an opportunity of living in their own way. I like his hobby passing well, however, which is a bigoted devotion to old English manners and customs; it jumps a little with my own humour, having as yet a lively and unsated curiosity about the ancient and genuine characteristics of my "fatherland."

There are some traits about the Squire's family also, which appear to me to be national. It is one of those old aristocratical families, which, I believe, are peculiar to England, and scarcely understood in other countries; that is to say, families of the ancient gentry, who, though destitute of titled rank, maintain a high ancestral pride; who look down upon all nobility of recent creation, and would consider it a sacrifice of dignity to merge the venerable name of their house in a modern title.

This feeling is very much fostered by the importance which they enjoy on their hereditary domains. The family mansion is an old manor-house, standing in a retired and beautiful part of Yorkshire. Its inhabitants have been always regarded through the surrounding country, as "the great ones of the earth;" and the little village near the hall looks up to the Squire with almost feudal homage. An old manor-house, and an old family of this kind, are rarely to be met with at the present day; and it is probably the peculiar humour of the Squire that has retained this secluded specimen of English housekeeping in something like the genuine old style.

I am again quartered in the panelled chamber, in the antique wing of the house. The prospect from my window, however, has quite a different aspect from that which it wore on my winter visit. Though early in the month of April, yet a few warm, sunshiny days have drawn forth the beauties of the spring, which, I think, are always most captivating on their first opening. The parterres of the old-fashioned garden are gay with flowers; and the gardener has brought out his exotics, and placed them along the stone

balustrades. The trees are clothed with green buds and tender leaves; when I throw open my jingling casement I smell the odour of mignonette, and hear the hum of the bees from the flowers against the sunny wall, with the varied song of the throstle, and the cheerful notes of the tuneful little wren.

While sojourning in this stronghold of old fashions, it is my intention to make occasional sketches of the scenes and characters before me. I would have it understood, however, that

I am not writing a novel, and have nothing of intricate plot, or marvellous adventure, to promise the reader. The Hall of which I treat has, for aught I know, neither trap-door, nor sliding-panel, nor donjon-keep: and indeed appears to have no mystery about it. The family is a worthy, well-meaning family, that, in all probability, will eat and drink, and go to bed, and get up regularly, from one end of my work to the

other; and the Squire is so kind-hearted an old gentleman, that I see no likelihood of his throwing any kind of distress in the way of the approaching nuptials. In a word, I cannot foresee a single extraordinary event that is likely to occur in the whole term of my sojourn at the hall.

I tell this honestly to the reader, lest when he find me dallying along, through everyday English scenes, he may hurry ahead, in hopes of meeting with some marvellous adventure farther on. I invite him, on the contrary, to ramble gently on with me, as he would saunter out into the fields, stopping occasionally to gather a flower, or listen to a bird, or admire a prospect, without any anxiety to arrive at the end of his career. Should I, however, in the course of my loiterings about this old mansion, see or hear anything curious, that might serve to vary the monotony of this everyday life, I shall not fail to report it for the reader's entertainment.

> For freshest wits I know will soon be wearie
> Of any book, how grave so e'er it be,
> Except it have odd matter, strange and merrie,
> Well-sauc'd with lies and glared all with glee.*

* Mirror for Magistrates.

THE BUSY MAN

> A decayed gentleman, who lives most upon his own mirth and my master's means, and much good do him with it. He does hold my master up with his stories, and songs, and catches, and such tricks, and jigs you would admire—he is with him now.
>
> *Jovial Crew.*

By no one has my return to the Hall been more heartily greeted than by Mr. Simon Bracebridge, or Master Simon, as the Squire most commonly calls him. I encountered him just as I entered the park, where he was breaking a pointer, and he received me with all the hospitable cordiality with which a man welcomes a friend to another one's house. I have already introduced him to the reader as a brisk old bachelor-looking little man; the wit and superannuated beau of a large family connection, and the Squire's factotum. I found him, as usual, full of bustle; with a thousand petty things to do, and persons to attend to, and in chirping good-humour; for there are few happier beings than a busy idler; that is to say, a man who is eternally busy about nothing.

I visited him, the morning after my arrival, in his chamber, which is in a remote corner of the mansion, as he says he likes to be to himself, and out of the way. He has fitted it up in his own taste, so that it is a perfect epitome of an old bachelor's notions of convenience and arrangement. The furniture is made up of odd pieces from all parts of the house, chosen on account of their suiting his notions, or fitting some corner of his apartment : and he is very eloquent in praise of an ancient elbow-chair, from which he takes occasion to digress into a censure on modern chairs, as having degenerated from the dignity and comfort of high-backed antiquity.

Adjoining to his room is a small cabinet, which he calls his study. Here are some hanging shelves, of his own construction, on which are several old works on hawking, hunting, and farriery, and a collection or two of poems and songs of the reign of Elizabeth, which he studies out of compliment to the Squire ; together with the Novelists' Magazine, the Sporting Magazine, the Racing Calendar, a volume or two of the Newgate Calendar, a book of peerage, and another of heraldry.

His sporting dresses hang on pegs in a small closet ; and about the walls of his apartment are hooks to hold his fishing-tackle, whips, spurs, and a favourite fowling-piece, curiously wrought and inlaid, which he inherits from his grandfather. He has also a couple of old single-keyed flutes, and a fiddle, which he has repeatedly patched and mended himself, affirming it to be a veritable Cremona : though I have never heard him extract a single note from it that was not enough to make one's blood run cold.

From this little nest his fiddle will often be heard, in the stillness of mid-day, drowsily sawing some long-forgotten tune ; for he prides himself on having a choice collection of good old English music, and will scarcely have anything to do with modern composers. The time, however, at which his musical powers are of most use, is now and then of an evening, when he plays for the children to dance in the hall, and he passes among them and the servants for a perfect Orpheus.

His chamber also bears evidence of his various avocations; there are half-copied sheets of music; designs for needlework; sketches of landscapes, very indifferently executed; a camera lucida; a magic lantern, for which he is endeavouring to paint glasses: in a word, it is the cabinet of a man of many accomplishments, who knows a little of everything, and does nothing well.

After I had spent some time in his apartment, admiring the ingenuity of his small inventions, he took me about the establishment, to visit the stables, dog-kennel, and other dependencies, in which he appeared like a general visiting the different quarters of his camp; as the Squire leaves the control of all these matters to him, when he is at the Hall. He inquired into the state of the horses; examined their feet; prescribed a drench for one, and bleeding for another; and then took me to look at his own horse, on the merits of which he dwelt with great prolixity, and which, I noticed, had the best stall in the stable.

After this I was taken to a new toy of his and the Squire's, which he termed the falconry, where there were several unhappy birds in durance, completing their education. Among the number was a fine falcon, which Master Simon had in especial training, and he told me that he would show me, in a few days, some rare sport of the good old-fashioned kind. In the course of our round, I noticed that the grooms, gamekeeper, whippers-

in, and other retainers, seemed all to be on somewhat of a familiar footing with Master Simon, and fond of having a joke with him, though it was evident they had great deference for his opinion in matters relating to their functions.

There was one exception, however, in a testy old huntsman, as hot as a pepper-corn ; a meagre, wiry old fellow, in a threadbare velvet jockey cap, and a pair of leather breeches, that, from much wear, shone as though they had been japanned. He was very contradictory and pragmatical, and apt, as I thought, to differ from Master Simon now and then, out of mere captiousness. This was particularly the case with respect to the treatment of the hawk, which the old man seemed to have under his peculiar care, and, according to Master Simon, was in a fair way to ruin : the latter had a vast deal to say about *casting*, and *imping*, and *gleaming*, and *enseaming*, and giving the hawk the *rangle*, which I saw was all heathen Greek to old Christy; but he maintained his point notwithstanding, and seemed to hold all his technical lore in utter disrespect.

I was surprised at the good humour with which Master Simon bore his contradictions, till he explained the matter to  me afterwards. Old Christy is the most ancient servant in the place, having lived among dogs and horses the greater part of a century, and been in the service of Mr. Bracebridge's father. He knows the pedigree of every horse on the place, and has bestrid the great-great-grandsires of most of them. He can give a circumstantial detail of every fox-hunt for the last sixty or seventy years, and has a history of every stag's head about the house, and every hunting trophy nailed to the door of the dog-kennel. All the present race have grown up under his eye, and humour him in his old age. He once attended the Squire to Oxford when he was a student there, and enlightened the whole university with his hunting lore. All this is enough to make the old man opinionated, since he finds, on all these matters of first-rate importance, he knows more than the rest of the world. Indeed, Master Simon had been his pupil, and acknowledges that he derived his first knowledge in hunting from the instructions of Christy; and I much question whether the old man does not still look upon him as rather a greenhorn.

On our return homewards, as we were crossing the lawn in front of the house, we heard the porter's bell ring at the lodge, and shortly afterwards a kind of cavalcade advanced slowly up the avenue. At sight of it my companion paused, considered for a moment, and then, making a sudden exclamation, hurried away to meet it. As it approached I discovered a fair, fresh-looking elderly lady, dressed in an old-fashioned riding habit, with a broad-brimmed white beaver hat, such as may be seen in Sir Joshua Reynolds' paintings. She rode a sleek white pony, and was followed by a footman in rich livery, mounted on an over-fed hunter. At a little distance in the rear came

an ancient cumbrous chariot, drawn by two very corpulent horses, driven by as corpulent a coachman, beside whom sat a page dressed in a fanciful green livery. Inside of the chariot was a starched prim personage, with a look somewhat between a lady's companion and a lady's maid, and two pampered curs that showed their ugly faces and barked out of each window.

There was a general turning out of the garrison to receive this new-comer. The Squire assisted her to alight, and saluted her affectionately; the fair Julia flew into her arms, and they embraced with the romantic fervour of boarding-school friends.

She was escorted into the house by Julia's lover, towards whom she showed distinguished favour; and a line of the old servants, who had collected in the hall, bowed most profoundly as she passed. I observed that Master Simon was most assiduous and devout in his attentions upon this old lady. He walked by the side of her pony up the avenue: and while she was receiving the salutations of the rest of the family, he took occasion to notice the fat coachman, to pat the sleek carriage-horses, and, above all, to say a civil word to my lady's gentlewoman, the prim, sour-looking vestal in the chariot.

I had no more of his company for the rest of the morning. He was swept off in the vortex that followed in the wake of this lady. Once indeed he paused for a moment, as he was hurrying on some errand of the good lady's, to let me know that this was Lady Lillycraft, a sister of the Squire's, of large fortune, which the captain would inherit, and that her estate lay in one of the best sporting counties in all England.

FAMILY SERVANTS

Verily old servants are the vouchers of worthy housekeeping. They are like rats in a mansion, or mites in a cheese, bespeaking the antiquity and fatness of their abode.

IN my casual anecdotes of the Hall, I may often be tempted to dwell on circumstances of a trite and ordinary nature, from their appearing to me illustrative of genuine national character. It seems to be the study of the Squire to adhere, as much as possible, to what he considers the old landmarks of English manners. His servants all understand his ways, and, for the most part, have been accustomed to them from infancy; so that, upon the whole, his household presents one of the few tolerable specimens that can now be met with, of the establishment of an English country gentleman of the old school. By the by, the servants are not the least characteristic part of the household; the housekeeper, for instance, has been born and brought up at the Hall, and has never been twenty miles from it; yet she has a stately air that would not disgrace a lady that had figured at the court of Queen Elizabeth.

I am half-inclined to think that she has caught it from living so much among the old family pictures. It may, however, be owing to a consciousness of her importance in the sphere in which she has always moved; for she is greatly respected in the neighbouring village, and among the farmers' wives, and has high authority in the household, ruling over the servants with quiet but undisputed sway.

She is a thin old lady, with blue eyes, and pointed nose and chin. Her dress is always the same as to fashion. She wears a small, well starched ruff, a laced stomacher, full petticoats,

and a gown festooned and open in front, which, on particular occasions, is of ancient silk, the legacy of some former dame of the family, or an inheritance from her mother, who was housekeeper before her. I have a reverence for these old garments, as I make no doubt they have figured about these apartments in days long past, when they have set off the charms of some peerless family beauty; and I have sometimes looked from the old housekeeper to the neighbouring portraits, to see whether I could not recognise her antiquated brocade in the dress of some one of those long-waisted dames that smile on me from the walls.

Her hair, which is quite white, is frizzed out in front, and she wears over it a small cap, nicely plaited and brought down under the chin. Her manners are simple and primitive, heightened a little by a proper dignity of station.

The Hall is her world, and the history of the family the only history she knows, excepting that which she has read in the Bible. She can give a biography of every portrait in the picture gallery, and is a complete family chronicle.

She is treated with great consideration by the Squire. Indeed, Master Simon tells me that there is a traditional anecdote current among the servants, of the Squire's having been seen kissing her in the picture-gallery, when they were both young. As, however, nothing further was ever noticed between them, the circumstance caused no great scandal; only she was observed to take to reading Pamela shortly afterwards, and refused the hand of the village innkeeper, whom she had previously smiled on.

The old butler, who was formerly footman, and a rejected admirer of hers, used to tell the anecdote now and then, at those little cabals that will occasionally take place among the most orderly servants, arising from the common propensity of the governed to talk against administration; but he has left it off, of late years, since he has risen into place, and shakes his head rebukingly when it is mentioned.

It is certain that the old lady will, to this day, dwell on the looks of the Squire when he was a young man at college; and she maintains that none of his sons can compare with their father when he was of their age, and was dressed out in his full suit of scarlet, with his hair craped and powdered, and his three-cornered hat.

She has an orphan niece, a pretty soft-hearted baggage,

named Phœbe Wilkins, who has been transplanted to the Hall within a year or two, and been nearly spoiled for any condition of life. She is a kind of attendant and companion of the fair Julia's; and from loitering about the young lady's apartments, reading scraps of novels, and inheriting second-hand finery, has become something between a waiting-maid and a slip-shod fine lady.

She is considered a kind of heiress among the servants, as she will inherit all her aunt's property; which, if report be true,

must be a round sum of good golden guineas, the accumulated wealth of two housekeepers' savings; not to mention the hereditary wardrobe, and the many little valuables and knick-knacks treasured up in the housekeeper's room. Indeed the old housekeeper has the reputation among the servants and the villagers of being passing rich; and there is a japanned chest of drawers and a large iron-bound coffer in her room, which are supposed by the housemaids to hold treasures of wealth.

The old lady is a great friend of Master Simon, who, indeed, pays a little court to her, as to a person high in authority; and they have many discussions on points of family history, in which, notwithstanding his extensive information, and pride of knowledge, he commonly admits her superior accuracy. He seldom returns to the Hall, after one of his visits to the other branches of the family, without bringing Mrs. Wilkins some remembrance from the ladies of the house where he has been staying.

Indeed all the children in the house look up to the old lady

with habitual respect and attachment, and she seems almost to consider them as her own, from their having grown up under her eye. The Oxonian, however, is her favourite, probably from being the youngest, though he is the most mischievous, and has been apt to play tricks upon her from boyhood.

I cannot help mentioning one little ceremony which, I believe, is peculiar to the Hall. After the cloth is removed at dinner, the old housekeeper sails into the room and stands behind the Squire's chair, when he fills her a glass of wine with his own hands, in which she drinks the health of the company in a truly respectful yet dignified manner, and then retires. The Squire received the custom from his father, and has always continued it.

There is a peculiar character about the servants of old English families that reside principally in the country. They have a quiet, orderly, respectful mode of doing their duties. They are always neat in their persons, and appropriately, and, if I may use the phrase, technically dressed; they move about the house without hurry or noise; there is nothing of the bustle of employment or the voice of command; nothing of that obtrusive housewifery that amounts to a torment. You are not persecuted by the process of making you comfortable; yet everything is done, and is done well. The work of the house is performed as if by magic, but it is the magic of system. Nothing is done by fits and starts, nor at awkward seasons; the whole goes on like well-oiled clockwork, where there is no noise nor jarring in its operations.

English servants, in general, are not treated with great indulgence, nor rewarded by many commendations; for the English are laconic and reserved towards their domestics; but an approving nod and kind word from master or mistress goes as far here as an excess of praise or indulgence elsewhere. Neither do servants exhibit any animated marks of affection to their employers; yet, though quiet, they are strong in their attachments; and the reciprocal regard of masters or servants, though not ardently expressed, is powerful and lasting in old English families.

The title of "an old family servant" carries with it a thousand kind associations in all parts of the world; and there is no claim upon the home-bred charities of the heart more irresistible than that of having been "born in the house." It is common to see gray-headed domestics of this kind attached to an English family of the "old school," who continue in it to the day of their death in the enjoyment of steady unaffected kindness, and the performance of faithful unofficious duty. I think such instances of attachment speak well for master and servant, and the frequency of them speaks well for national character.

These observations, however, hold good only with families of the description I have mentioned, and with such as are somewhat retired, and pass the greater part of their time in the country. As to the powdered menials that throng the walls of fashionable town residences, they equally reflect the character of the establishments to which they belong; and I know no more complete epitomes of dissolute heartlessness and pampered inutility.

But the good "old family servant!"—The one who has always been linked, in idea, with the home of our heart; who has led us to school in the days of prattling childhood; who has been the confidant of our boyish cares, and schemes, and enterprises; who has hailed us as we came home at vacations, and been the promoter of all our holiday sports; who, when we, in wandering manhood, have left the paternal roof, and only return thither at intervals, will welcome us with a joy inferior only to that of our parents; who, now grown gray and infirm with age, still totters about the house of our fathers in fond and faithful servitude; who claims us, in a manner, as his own; and hastens with querulous eagerness to anticipate his fellow domestics in waiting upon us at table; and who, when we retire at night to the chamber that still goes by our name, will linger about the room to have one more kind look, and one more pleasant word about times that are past—who does not experience towards such a being a feeling of almost filial affection?

I have met with several instances of epitaphs on the gravestones of such valuable domestics, recorded with the simple truth of natural feeling. I have two before me at this moment;

one copied from a tombstone of a churchyard in Warwickshire :

"Here lieth the body of Joseph Batte, confidential servant to George Birch, Esq. of Hampstead Hall. His grateful friend

and master caused this inscription to be written in memory of his discretion, fidelity, diligence, and continence. He died (a bachelor) aged 84, having lived 44 years in the same family."

The other was taken from a tombstone in Eltham churchyard :

"Here lie the remains of Mr. James Tappy, who departed this life on the 8th of September 1818, aged 84, after a faithful service of 60 years in one family; by each individual of which he lived respected, and died lamented by the sole survivor."

Few monuments, even of the illustrious, have given me the glow about the heart that I felt while copying this honest epitaph in the churchyard of Eltham. I sympathised with this "sole survivor" of a family, mourning over the grave of the faithful follower of his race, who had been, no doubt, a living memento of the times and friends that had passed away: and in considering this record of long and devoted services, I called to mind the touching speech of old Adam in "As You Like It," when tottering after the youthful son of his ancient master:

> "Master, go on, and I will follow thee
> To the last gasp, with love and loyalty!"

NOTE.—I cannot but mention a tablet which I have seen somewhere in the chapel of Windsor Castle, put up by the late king to the memory of a family servant, who had been a faithful attendant of his lamented daughter, the Princess Amelia. George III. possessed much of the strong domestic feeling of the old English country gentleman; and it is an incident curious in monumental history, and creditable to the human heart,—a monarch erecting a monument in honour of the humble virtues of a menial.

THE WIDOW

She was so charitable and pitious
She would weep if that she saw a mous
Caught in a trap, if it were dead or bled :
Of small hounds had she, that she fed
With rost flesh, milke, and wastel bread :
But sore wept she if any of them were dead,
Or if man smote them with a yard smart.
         CHAUCER.

NOTWITHSTANDING the whimsical parade made by Lady Lillycraft on her arrival, she has none of the petty stateliness that I had imagined ; but, on the contrary, she has a degree of nature, and simple-heartedness, if I may use the phrase, that mingles well with her old-fashioned manners and harmless ostentation. She dresses in rich silks, with long waist ; she rouges considerably, and her hair, which is nearly white, is frizzled out, and put up with pins. Her face is pitted with the small-pox, but the delicacy of her features shows that she may once have been beautiful; and she has a very fair and well-shaped hand and arm, of which, if I mistake not, the good lady is still a little vain.

I have had the curiosity to gather a few particulars concerning her. She was a great belle in town between thirty and forty years since, and reigned for two seasons with all the insolence of beauty, refusing several excellent offers; when, unfortunately, she was robbed of her charms and her lovers by an attack of the small-pox. She retired immediately into the country, where she some time after inherited an estate, and married a baronet, a former admirer, whose passion had suddenly revived; "having," as he said, "always loved her mind rather than her person."

The baronet did not enjoy her mind and fortune above six months, and had scarcely grown very tired of her, when he broke his neck in a fox-chase and left her free, rich, and disconsolate. She has remained on her estate in the country ever since, and has never shown any desire to return to town, and revisit the scene of her early triumphs and fatal malady. All her favourite recollections, however, revert to that short period of her youthful beauty. She has no idea of town but as it was at that time; and continually forgets that the place and people must have changed materially in the course of nearly half a century. She will often speak of the toasts of those days as if still reigning; and, until very recently, used to talk with delight of the royal family, and the beauty of the young princes and princesses. She cannot be brought to think of the present king otherwise than as an elegant young man, rather wild, but who danced a minuet divinely; and before he came to the crown, would often mention him as the "sweet young prince."

She talks also of the walks in Kensington Gardens, where the gentlemen appeared in gold-laced coats and cocked hats, and the ladies in hoops, and swept so proudly along the grassy avenues; and she thinks the ladies let themselves sadly down in their dignity when they gave up cushioned head-dresses and

high-heeled shoes. She has much to say too of the officers who were in the train of her admirers; and speaks familiarly of many wild young blades, that are now, perhaps, hobbling about watering-places with crutches and gouty shoes.

Whether the taste the good lady had of matrimony discouraged her or not, I cannot say; but, though her merits and her riches have attracted many suitors, she has never been tempted to venture again into the happy state. This is singular too, for she seems of a most soft and susceptible heart: is always talking of love and connubial felicity; and is a great stickler for old-fashioned gallantry, devoted attentions, and eternal constancy, on the part of the gentlemen. She lives, however, after her own taste. Her house, I am told, must have been built and furnished about the time of Sir Charles Grandison; everything about it is somewhat formal and stately; but has been softened down into a degree of voluptuousness, characteristic of an old lady very tender-hearted and romantic, and that loves her ease. The cushions of the great arm-chairs, and wide sofas, almost bury you when you sit down on them. Flowers of the most rare and delicate kind are placed about the rooms and on little japanned stands; and sweet bags lie about the tables and mantelpieces. The house is full of pet dogs, Angola cats, and singing birds, who are as carefully waited upon as she is herself.

She is dainty in her living, and a little of an epicure, living on white meats, and little lady-like dishes, though her servants have substantial old English fare, as their looks bear witness. Indeed, they are so indulged, that they are all spoiled, and when they lose their present place they will be fit for no other. Her ladyship is one of those easy tempered beings that are always doomed to be much liked, but ill served, by their domestics, and cheated by all the world.

Much of her time is passed in reading novels, of which she has a most extensive library, and has a constant supply from the publishers in town. Her erudition in this line of literature is immense: she has kept pace with the press for half a century. Her mind is stuffed with love tales of all kinds, from the stately amours of the old books of Chivalry, down to the last blue-covered romance, reeking from the press: though she evidently gives the preference to those that came out in the days of her youth, and when she was first in love. She maintains that there are no novels written nowadays equal to Pamela and Sir Charles Grandison; and she places the Castle of Otranto at the head of all romances.

She does a vast deal of good in her neighbourhood, and is

imposed upon by every beggar in the county. She is the
benefactress of a village adjoining to her estate, and takes a
special interest in all its love affairs. She knows of every
courtship that is going on; every love-lorn damsel is sure to

find a patient listener and sage adviser in her ladyship. She
takes great pains to reconcile all love quarrels, and should any
faithless swain persist in his inconstancy, he is sure to draw
on himself the good lady's violent indignation.

I have learned these particulars partly from Frank Bracebridge and partly from Master Simon. I am now able to
account for the assiduous attention of the latter to her ladyship.
Her house is one of his favourite resorts, where he is a very
important personage. He makes her a visit of business once a
year, when he looks into all her affairs; which, as she is no
manager, are apt to get into confusion. He examines the
books of the overseer, and shoots about the estate, which, he
says, is well stocked with game notwithstanding that it is
poached by all the vagabonds in the neighbourhood.

THE WIDOW

It is thought, as I before hinted, that the captain will inherit the greater part of her property, having always been her chief favourite; for, in fact, she is partial to a red coat. She has now come to the Hall to be present at his nuptials, having a great disposition to interest herself in all matters of love and matrimony.

THE LOVERS

Rise up, my love, my fair one, and come away; for lo the winter is past, the rain is over and gone; the flowers appear on the earth, the time of the singing of birds is come, and the voice of the turtle is heard in the land.

Song of Solomon.

To a man who is a little of a philosopher, and a bachelor to boot; and who, by dint of some experience in the follies of life, begins to look with a learned eye upon the ways of man and eke of woman; to such a man, I say, there is something very entertaining in noticing the conduct of a pair of young lovers. It may not be as grave and scientific a study as the loves of the plants, but it is certainly as interesting.

I have therefore derived much pleasure, since my arrival at the Hall, from observing the fair Julia and her lover. She has all the delightful blushing consciousness of an artless girl, inexperienced in coquetry, who has made her first conquest; while the captain regards her with that mixture of fondness and exultation, with which a youthful lover is apt to contemplate so beauteous a prize.

I observed them yesterday in the garden, advancing along one of the retired walks. The sun was shining with delicious warmth, making great masses of bright verdure, and deep blue shade. The cuckoo, that "harbinger of spring," was faintly

'The fair Julia was leaning on her lover's arm, listening to his conversation.'

heard from a distance; the thrush piped from the hawthorn, and the yellow butterflies sported, and toyed, and coquetted in the air.

The fair Julia was leaning on her lover's arm, listening to his conversation, with her eyes cast down, a soft blush on her cheek, and a quiet smile on her lips, while in the hand that hung negligently by her side was a bunch of flowers. In this way they were sauntering slowly along, and when I considered them, and the scene in which they were moving, I could not but think it a thousand pities that the season should ever change, or that young people should ever grow older, or that blossoms should give way to fruit, or that lovers should ever get married.

From what I have gathered of family anecdote, I understand that the fair Julia is the daughter of a favourite college friend of the Squire; who, after leaving Oxford, had entered the army, and served for many years in India, where he was mortally wounded in a skirmish with the natives. In his last moments he had, with a faltering pen, recommended his wife and daughter to the kindness of his early friend.

The widow and her child returned to England helpless, and almost hopeless. When Mr. Bracebridge received accounts of their situation, he hastened to their relief. He reached them just in time to soothe the last moments of the mother, who was dying of a consumption, and to make her happy in the assurance that her child should never want a protector.

The good Squire returned with his prattling charge to his stronghold, where he has brought her up with a tenderness truly paternal. As he has taken some pains to superintend her education, and form her taste, she has grown up with many of his notions, and considers him the wisest as well as the best of men. Much of her time, too, has been passed with Lady Lillycraft, who has instructed her in the manners of the old school, and enriched her mind with all kinds of novels and romances. Indeed, her ladyship has had a great hand in promoting the match between Julia and the captain, having had them together at her country seat the moment she found there was an attachment growing up between them; the good lady being never so happy as when she has a pair of turtles cooing about her.

I have been pleased to see the fondness with which the fair Julia is regarded by the old servants of the Hall. She has been a pet with them from childhood, and every one seems to lay some claim to her education: so that it is no wonder that she should be extremely accomplished. The gardener taught her to rear flowers, of which she is extremely fond. Old Christy, the pragmatical huntsman, softens when she approaches; and as she sits lightly and gracefully in her saddle, claims the merit of having taught her to ride; while the housekeeper, who almost looks upon her as a daughter, intimates that she first gave her an insight into the mysteries of the toilet, having been dressing-maid in her young days to the late Mrs. Bracebridge. I am inclined to credit this last claim, as I have noticed that the dress of the young lady had an air of the old school, though managed with native taste, and that her hair was put up very much in the style of Sir Peter Lely's portraits in the picture-gallery.

Her very musical attainments partake of this old-fashioned character, and most of her songs are such as are not at the present day to be found on the piano of a modern performer. I have, however, seen so much of modern fashions, modern accomplishments, and modern fine ladies, that I relish this tinge of antiquated style in so young and lovely a girl; and I have had as much pleasure in hearing her warble one of the old songs of Herrick, or Carew, or Suckling, adapted to some simple old melody, as I have had from listening to a lady amateur skylark it up and down through the finest bravura of Rossini or Mozart.

We have very pretty music in the evenings, occasionally, between her and the captain, assisted sometimes by Master Simon, who scrapes, dubiously, on his violin; being very apt to get out, and to halt a note or two in the rear. Sometimes he even thrums a little on the piano, and takes a part in a trio, in which his voice can generally be distinguished by a certain quavering tone, and an occasional false note.

I was praising the fair Julia's performance to him after one of her songs, when I found he took to himself the whole credit of having formed her musical taste, assuring me that she was very apt; and, indeed, summing up her whole character in his knowing way, by adding, that "she was a very nice girl, and had no nonsense about her."

FAMILY RELIQUES

>My Infelice's face, her brow, her eye,
>The dimple on her cheek and such sweet skill
>Hath from the cunning workman's pencil flown,
>These lips look fresh and lovely as her own.
>False colours last after the true be dead.
>Of all the roses grafted on her cheeks,
>Of all the graces dancing in her eyes,
>Of all the music set upon her tongue,
>Of all that was past woman's excellence
>In her white bosom; look, a painted board,
>Circumscribes all!　　　　　　　　DEKKER.

AN old English family mansion is a fertile subject for study. It abounds with illustrations of former times, and traces of the tastes, and humours, and manners of successive generations. The alterations and additions, in different styles of architecture; the furniture, plate, pictures, hangings; the warlike and sporting implements of different ages and fancies; all furnish food for curious and amusing speculation. As the Squire is very careful in collecting and preserving all family reliques, the Hall is full of remembrances of this kind. In looking about the establishment, I can picture to myself the characters and habits that have prevailed at different eras of the family history. I have mentioned on a former occasion the armour of the crusader which hangs up in the Hall. There are also several jack-boots, with enormously thick soles and high heels, that belonged to a set of cavaliers, who filled the Hall with the din and stir of arms during the time of the Covenanters. A number of enormous drinking vessels of antique fashion, with huge Venice glasses, and green hock glasses, with the apostles in relief on them, remain as monuments of a generation or two of hard livers, that led a life of roaring revelry, and first introduced the gout into the family.

I shall pass over several more such indications of temporary tastes of the Squire's predecessors; but I cannot forbear to notice a pair of antlers in the great hall, which is one of the trophies of a hard-riding squire of former times, who was the Nimrod of these parts. There are many traditions of his wonderful feats in hunting still existing, which are related by old Christy, the huntsman, who gets exceedingly nettled if they are in the least doubted. Indeed, there is a frightful chasm, a few miles from the Hall, which goes by the name of the Squire's Leap, from his having cleared it in the ardour of the chase; there can be no doubt of the fact, for old Christy shows the very dints of the horse's hoofs on the rocks on each side of the chasm.

Master Simon holds the memory of this squire in great veneration, and has a number of extraordinary stories to tell concerning him, which he repeats at all hunting dinners; and I am told that they wax more and more marvellous the older they grow. He has also a pair of Ripon spurs which belonged to this mighty hunter of yore, and which he only wears on particular occasions.

The place, however, which abounds most with mementoes of past times, is the picture-gallery; and there is something strangely pleasing, though melancholy, in considering the long rows of portraits which compose the greater part of the collection. They furnish a kind of narrative of the lives of the family worthies, which I am enabled to read with the assistance of the venerable housekeeper, who is the family chronicler, prompted occasionally by Master Simon. There is the progress of a fine lady, for instance, through a variety of portraits. One represents her as a little girl, with a long waist and hoop, holding a kitten in her arms, and ogling the spectator out of the corners of her eyes, as if she could not turn her head. In another we find her in the freshness of youthful beauty, when she was a celebrated belle, and so hard-hearted as to cause several unfortunate gentlemen to run desperate and write bad poetry. In another she is depicted as a stately dame, in the maturity of her charms; next to the portrait of her husband, a gallant colonel in full-bottomed wig and gold-laced hat, who was killed abroad; and, finally, her monument is in the church, the spire of which may be seen from the window, where her effigy is carved in marble, and represents her as a venerable dame of seventy-six.

In like manner I have followed some of the family great men, through a series of pictures, from early boyhood to the robe of dignity, or truncheon of command, and so on by degrees until they were gathered up in the common repository, the neighbouring church.

There is one group that particularly interested me. It consisted of four sisters of nearly the same age, who flourished about a century since, and, if I may judge from their portraits, were extremely beautiful. I can imagine what a scene of gaiety and romance this old mansion must have been when they were in the heyday of their charms; when they passed like beautiful visions through its halls, or stepped daintily to music in the revels and dances of the cedar gallery; or printed, with delicate feet, the velvet verdure of these lawns. How must they have been looked up to with mingled love, and pride, and reverence, by the old family servants; and followed by almost painful

admiration by the aching eyes of rival admirers! How must melody, and song, and tender serenade, have breathed about these courts, and their echoes whispered to the loitering tread of lovers! How must these very turrets have made the hearts of the young galliards thrill as they first discerned them from afar, rising from among the trees, and pictured to themselves the beauties casketed like gems within these walls! Indeed I have discovered about the place several faint records of this reign of love and romance, when the Hall was a kind of Court of Beauty. Several of the old romances in the library have marginal notes expressing sympathy and approbation, where there are long speeches extolling ladies' charms, or protesting eternal fidelity, or bewailing the cruelty of some tyrannical fair one. The interviews, and declarations, and parting scenes of tender lovers, also bear the marks of having been frequently read, and are scored, and marked with notes of admiration, and have initials written on the margins; most of which annotations have the day of the month and year annexed to them. Several of the windows, too, have scraps of poetry engraved on them with diamonds, taken from the writings of the fair Mrs. Phillips, the once celebrated Orinda. Some of these seem to have been inscribed by lovers: and others, in a delicate and unsteady hand, and a little inaccurate in the spelling, have evidently been written by the young ladies themselves, or by female friends, who had been on visits to the Hall. Mrs. Phillips seems to have been their favourite author, and they have distributed the names of her heroes and heroines among their circle of intimacy. Sometimes, in a male hand, the verse bewails the cruelty of beauty and the sufferings of constant love; while in a female hand it prudishly confines itself to lamenting the parting of female friends.

The bow-window of my bedroom, which has, doubtless, been inhabited by one of these beauties, has several of these inscriptions. I have one at this moment before my eyes called "Camilla parting with Leonora:"

> "How perished is the joy that's past,
> The present how unsteady!
> What comfort can be great, and last,
> When this is gone already!"

And close by it is another, written, perhaps, by some adventurous lover, who had stolen into the lady's chamber during her absence.

"THEODOSIUS TO CAMILLA.

I'd rather in your favour live,
　Than in a lasting name :
And much a greater rate would give
　For happiness than fame.

THEODOSIUS. 1700."

When I look at these faint records of gallantry and tenderness; when I contemplate the fading portraits of these beautiful girls, and think, too, that they have long since bloomed, reigned, grown old, died, and passed away, and with them all their graces, their triumphs, their rivalries, their admirers; the whole empire of love and pleasure in which they ruled—"all dead, all buried, all forgotten," I find a cloud of melancholy stealing

over the present gaieties around me. I was gazing, in a musing mood, this very morning, at the portrait of the lady whose husband was killed abroad, when the fair Julia entered the gallery, leaning on the arm of the captain. The sun shone through the row of windows on her as she passed along, and she seemed to beam out each time into brightness, and relapse into shade, until the door at the bottom of the gallery closed after her. I felt a sadness of heart at the idea, that this was an emblem of her lot: a few more years of sunshine and shade, and all this life, and loveliness, and enjoyment, will have ceased, and nothing be left to commemorate this beautiful being but one more perishable portrait; to awaken, perhaps, the trite speculations of some future loiterer, like myself, when I and my scribblings shall have lived through our brief existence, and been forgotten.

AN OLD SOLDIER

I've worn some leather out abroad; let out a heathen soul or two; fed this good sword with the black blood of pagan Christians; converted a few individuals with it.—But let that pass.

The Ordinary.

THE Hall was thrown into some little agitation, a few days since, by the arrival of General Harbottle. He had been expected for several days, and had been looked for rather impatiently by several of the family. Master Simon assured me that I would like the general hugely, for he was a blade of the old school, and an excellent table companion. Lady Lillycraft, also, appeared to be somewhat fluttered, on the morning of the general's arrival, for he had been one of her early admirers; and she recollected him only as a dashing young ensign, just come upon the town. She actually spent an hour longer at her toilet, and made her appearance, with her hair uncommonly frizzled and powdered, and an additional quantity of rouge. She was evidently a little surprised and shocked, therefore, at finding the little dashing ensign transformed into a corpulent old general, with a double chin, though it was a perfect picture to witness their salutations; the graciousness of her profound curtsy, and the air of the old school with which the general took off his hat, swayed it gently in his hand, and bowed his powdered head.

All this bustle and anticipation has caused me to study the general with a little more attention than, perhaps, I should otherwise have done; and the few days that he has already passed at the Hall have enabled me, I think, to furnish a tolerable likeness of him to the reader.

He is, as Master Simon observed, a soldier of the old school, with powdered head, side locks, and pigtail. His face is shaped like the stern of a Dutch man-of-war, narrow at top, and wide at bottom, with full rosy cheeks and a double chin; so that, to use the cant of the day, his organs of eating may be said to be powerfully developed.

The general, though a veteran, has seen very little active service, except the taking of Seringapatam, which forms an era in his history. He wears a large emerald in his bosom, and a diamond on his finger, which he got on that occasion, and whoever is unlucky enough to notice either, is sure to involve himself in the whole history of the siege. To judge from the general's conversation, the taking of Seringapatam is the most important affair that has occurred for the last century.

On the approach of warlike times on the Continent, he was rapidly promoted to get him out of the way of younger officers of merit; until, having been hoisted to the rank of general, he was quietly laid on the shelf. Since that time his campaigns have been principally confined to watering-places; where he drinks the waters for a slight touch of the liver which he got in India; and plays whist with old dowagers, with whom he has flirted in his younger days. Indeed he talks of all the fine women of the last half-century, and, according to hints which he now and then drops, has enjoyed the particular smiles of many of them.

He has seen considerable garrison duty, and can speak of almost every place famous for good quarters, and where the inhabitants give good dinners. He is a diner-out of the first-rate currency, when in town; being invited to one place because he has been seen at another. In the same way he is invited about the country seats, and can describe half the seats in the

kingdom, from actual observation; nor is any one better versed in court gossip, and the pedigrees and intermarriages of the nobility.

As the general is an old bachelor and an old beau, and there are several ladies at the Hall, especially his quondam flame Lady Jocelyne, he is put rather upon his gallantry. He commonly passes some time, therefore, at his toilet, and takes the field at a late hour every morning, with his hair dressed out and powdered, and a rose in his button-hole. After he has breakfasted, he walks up and down the terrace in the sunshine, humming an air, and hemming between every stave, carrying one hand behind his back, and with the other touching his cane to the ground and then raising it up to his shoulder. Should he, in these morning promenades, meet any of the elder ladies of the family, as he frequently does Lady Lillycraft, his hat is immediately in his hand, and it is enough to remind one of those courtly groups of ladies and gentlemen, in old prints of Windsor Terrace or Kensington Gardens.

He talks frequently about "the service," and is fond of humming the old song,

> "Why, soldiers, why,
>   Should we be melancholy, boys?
> Why, soldiers, why,
>   Whose business 'tis to die!"

I cannot discover, however, that the general has ever run any great risk of dying, excepting from an apoplexy, or indigestion. He criticises all the battles on the Continent, and discusses the merits of the commanders, but never fails to bring the conversation ultimately to Tippoo Saib and Seringapatam. I am told that the general was a perfect champion at drawing-rooms, parades, and watering-places, during the late war, and was looked to with hope and confidence by many an old lady, when labouring under the terror of Buonaparte's invasion.

He is thoroughly loyal, and attends punctually on levees when in town. He has treasured up many remarkable sayings of the late king, particularly one which the king made to him on a field day, complimenting him on the excellence of his horse. He extols the whole royal family, but especially the present king, whom he pronounces the most perfect gentleman and best whist-player in Europe. The general swears rather more than is the fashion of the present day; but it was the mode of the old school. He is, however, very strict in religious matters, and a staunch churchman. He repeats the responses very loudly in church, and is emphatical in praying for the king and royal family.

At table his loyalty waxes very fervent with his second bottle, and the song of "God save the King" puts him into a perfect ecstasy. He is amazingly well contented with the present state of things, and apt to get a little impatient at any talk about national ruin and agricultural distress. He says he has travelled about the country as much as any man, and has met with nothing but prosperity; and to confess the truth, a great part of his time is spent in visiting from one country-seat to another, and riding about the parks of his friends. "They talk of public distress," said the general this day to me, at dinner, as he smacked a glass of rich burgundy, and cast his eyes about the ample board; "they talk of public distress, but where do we find it, sir? I see none. I see no reason any one has to complain. Take my word for it, sir, this talk about public distress is all humbug!"

THE WIDOW'S RETINUE

Little dogs and all!—Lear.

In giving an account of the arrival of Lady Lillycraft at the Hall, I ought to have mentioned the entertainment which I derived from witnessing the unpacking of her carriage and the disposing of her retinue. There is something extremely amusing to me in the number of factitious wants, the loads of imaginary conveniences, but real incumbrances, with which the luxurious are apt to burden themselves. I like to watch the whimsical stir and display about one of these petty progresses. The number of robustious footmen and retainers of all kinds bustling about, with looks of infinite gravity and importance, to do almost nothing. The number of heavy trunks and parcels, and handboxes, belonging to my lady; and the solicitude exhibited about some humble, odd-looking box by my lady's maid; the cushions piled in the carriage to make a soft seat still softer; and to prevent the dreaded possibility of a jolt; the smelling-bottles, the cordials, the baskets of biscuit and fruit; the new publications; all provided to guard against hunger, fatigue, or ennui; the led horses to vary the mode of travelling; and all this preparation and parade to move, perhaps, some very good-for-nothing personage about a little space of earth!

I do not mean to apply the latter part of these observations to Lady Lillycraft, for whose simple kind-heartedness I have a very great respect, and who is really a most amiable and worthy being. I cannot refrain, however, from mentioning some of the motley retinue she has brought with her; and which, indeed, bespeak the overflowing kindness of her nature, which requires her to be surrounded with objects on which to lavish it.

In the first place, her ladyship has a pampered coachman, with a red face, and cheeks that hang down like dew-laps. He evidently domineers over her a little with respect to the fat horses; and only drives out when he thinks proper, and when he thinks it will be "good for the cattle."

She has a favourite page to attend upon her person; a handsome boy of about twelve years of age, but a mischievous varlet, very much spoiled, and in a fair way to be good for nothing. He is dressed in green, with a profusion of gold cord and gilt buttons about his clothes. She always has one or two attendants of the kind, who are replaced by others as soon as they grow to fourteen years of age. She has brought two dogs with her also, out of a number of pets which she maintains at home. One is a fat spaniel, called Zephyr— though heaven defend me from such a zephyr! He is fed out of all shape and comfort; his eyes are nearly strained out of his head; he wheezes with corpulency, and cannot walk without great difficulty. The other is a little, old, gray-muzzled curmudgeon, with an unhappy eye, that kindles like a coal if you only look at him; his nose turns up; his mouth is drawn into wrinkles, so as to show his teeth; in short, he has altogether the look of a dog far gone in misanthropy, and totally sick of the world. When he walks, he has his tail curled up so tight that it seems to lift his feet from the ground; and he seldom makes use of more than three legs at a time, keeping the other drawn up as a reserve. This last wretch is called Beauty.

These dogs are full of elegant ailments unknown to vulgar dogs; and are petted and nursed by Lady Lillycraft with the tenderest kindness. They are pampered and fed with delicacies by their fellow-minion, the page; but their stomachs are often weak and out of order, so that they cannot eat; though I have now and then seen the page give them a mischievous pinch or thwack over the head when his mistress was not by. They have cushions for their express use, on which they lie before the fire, and yet are apt to shiver and moan if there is the least draught of air. When any one enters the room they make a most tyrannical barking, that is absolutely deafening. They are insolent to all the other dogs of the establishment. There is a noble staghound, a great favourite of the Squire's, who is a privileged visitor to the parlour; but the moment he makes his appearance, these intruders fly at him with furious rage; and I have admired the sovereign indifference and contempt with which he seems to look down upon his puny assailants. When her ladyship drives out, these dogs are generally carried with her to take the air; when they look out of each window of the carriage, and bark at all vulgar pedestrian dogs. These dogs are a continual source of misery to the household: as

they are always in the way, they every now and then get their toes trod on, and then there is a yelping on their part, and a loud lamentation on the part of their mistress, that fills the room with clamour and confusion.

Lastly, there is her ladyship's waiting-gentlewoman, Mrs. Hannah, a prim, pragmatical old maid; one of the most intolerable and intolerant virgins that ever lived. She has kept her virtue by her until it has turned sour, and now every word and look smacks of verjuice. She is the very opposite to her mistress, for one hates, and the other loves, all mankind. How they first came together I cannot imagine, but they have lived together for many years; and the abigail's temper being tart and encroaching, and her ladyship's easy and yielding, the former has got the complete upper hand, and tyrannises over the good lady in secret.

Lady Lillycraft now and then complains of it, in great confidence, to her friends, but hushes up the subject immediately, if Mrs. Hannah makes her appearance. Indeed, she has been so accustomed to be attended by her, that she thinks she could not do without her; though one great study of her life is to keep Mrs. Hannah in good-humour, by little presents and kindnesses.

Master Simon has a most devout abhorrence, mingled with awe, for this ancient spinster. He told me the other day, in a whisper, that she was a cursed brimstone—in fact, he added another epithet, which I would not repeat for the world. I have remarked, however, that he is always extremely civil to her when they meet.

READY-MONEY JACK

>   My purse, it is my privy wyfe,
>   This song I dare both syng and say,
>   It keepeth men from grievous stryfe
>   When every man for hymself shall pay.
>   As I ryde in ryche array
>   For gold and sylver men wyll me floryshe;
>   By thys matter I dare well saye,
>   Ever gramercy myne owne purse.
>
>   *Book of Hunting.*

ON the skirts of the neighbouring village there lives a kind of small potentate, who, for aught I know, is a representative of one of the most ancient legitimate lines of the present day; for the empire over which he reigns has belonged to his family time out of mind. His territories comprise a considerable number of good fat acres; and his seat of power is an old farm-house, where he enjoys, unmolested, the stout oaken chair of his ancestors. The personage to whom I allude is a sturdy old yeoman of the name of John Tibbets, or rather Ready-Money Jack Tibbets, as he is called throughout the neighbourhood.

The first place where he attracted my attention was in the churchyard on Sunday; where he sat on a tombstone after service, with his hat a little on one side, holding forth to a small circle of auditors, and, as I presumed, expounding the law and the prophets, until, on drawing a little nearer, I found he was only expatiating on the merits of a brown horse. He presented so faithful a picture of a substantial English yeoman, such as he is often described in books, heightened, indeed, by some little finery peculiar to himself, that I could not but take note of his whole appearance.

He was between fifty and sixty, of a strong muscular frame, and at least six feet high, with a physiognomy as grave as a lion's, and set off with short, curling, iron-gray locks. His shirt-collar was turned down, and displayed a neck covered with the same short, curling, gray hair; and he wore a coloured silk neckcloth, tied very loosely, and tucked in at the bosom, with a green paste brooch on the knot. His coat was of dark-green cloth, with silver buttons, on each of which was engraved a stag, with his own name, John Tibbets, underneath. He had an inner waistcoat of figured chintz, between which and his coat was another of scarlet cloth unbuttoned. His breeches were also left unbuttoned at the knees, not from any slovenliness, but to show a broad pair of scarlet garters. His stockings were blue, with white clocks; he wore large silver shoe-buckles; a broad paste buckle in his hatband; his sleeve buttons were gold seven-shilling pieces; and he had two or three guineas hanging as ornaments to his watch-chain.

On making some inquiries about him, I gathered that he was descended from a line of farmers that had always lived on the same spot, and owned the same property; and that half of the churchyard was taken up with the tombstones of his race. He has all his life been an important character in the place.

When a youngster, he was one of the most roaring blades of the neighbourhood. No one could match him at wrestling, pitching the bar, cudgel play, and other athletic exercises. Like the renowned Pinner of Wakefield, he was the village champion; carried off the prize at all the fairs, and threw his gauntlet at the country round. Even to this day the old people talk of his prowess, and undervalue, in comparison, all heroes of the green that have succeeded him; nay, they say that if Ready-Money Jack were to take the field even now, there is no one could stand before him.

When Jack's father died, the neighbours shook their heads, and predicted that young Hopeful would soon make way with the old homestead; but Jack falsified all their predictions. The moment he succeeded to the paternal farm he assumed a new character; took a wife; attended resolutely to his affairs, and became an industrious, thrifty farmer. With the family property he inherited a set of old family maxims, to which he steadily adhered. He saw to everything himself; put his own hand to the plough; worked hard; ate heartily; slept soundly; paid for everything in cash down; and never danced except he could do it to the music of his own money in both pockets. He has never been without a hundred or two pounds in gold by him, and never allows a debt to stand unpaid. This has gained him his current name, of which, by the by, he is a little proud; and has caused him to be looked upon as a very wealthy man by all the village.

Notwithstanding his thrift, however, he has never denied himself the amusements of life, but has taken a share in every passing pleasure. It is his maxim, that "he that works hard can afford to play." He is, therefore, an attendant at all the country fairs and wakes, and has signalised himself by feats of strength and prowess on every village green in the shire. He often makes his appearance at horse-races, and sports his half-guinea and even his guinea at a time; keeps a good horse for his own riding, and to this day is fond of following the hounds and is generally in at the death. He keeps up the rustic

revels, and hospitalities too, for which his paternal farm-house has always been noted ; has plenty of good cheer and dancing at harvest-home, and above all, keeps the "merry night,"* as it is termed at Christmas.

With all his love of amusement, however, Jack is by no means a boisterous jovial companion. He is seldom known to laugh even in the midst of his gaiety ; but maintains the same grave, lion-like demeanour. He is very slow at comprehending a joke ; and is apt to sit puzzling at it, with a perplexed look, while the rest of the company is in a roar. This gravity has, perhaps, grown on him with the growing weight of his character ; for he is gradually rising into patriarchal dignity in his native place. Though he no longer takes an active part in athletic sports, yet he always presides at them, and is appealed to on all occasions as umpire. He maintains the peace on the village-green at holiday games, and quells all brawls and quarrels by collaring the parties and shaking them heartily, if refractory. No one ever pretends to raise a hand against him, or to contend against his decisions ; the young men having grown up in

---

* MERRY NIGHT; a rustic merry-making in a farm-house about Christmas, common in some parts of Yorkshire. There is abundance of homely fare, tea, cakes, fruit, and ale ; various feats of agility, amusing games, romping, dancing, and kissing withal. They commonly break up at midnight.

habitual awe of his prowess, and in implicit deference to him as the champion and lord of the green.

He is a regular frequenter of the village inn, the landlady having been a sweetheart of his in early life, and he having always continued on kind terms with her. He seldom, however, drinks anything but a draught of ale; smokes his pipe, and pays his reckoning before leaving the tap-room. Here he "gives his little senate laws;" decides bets, which are very

generally referred to him; determines upon the characters and qualities of horses; and indeed plays now and then the part of a judge, in settling petty disputes between neighbours, which otherwise might have been nursed by country attorneys into tolerable lawsuits. Jack is very candid and impartial in his decisions, but he has not a head to carry a long argument, and is very apt to get perplexed and out of patience if there is much pleading. He generally breaks through the argument with a strong voice, and brings matters to a summary conclusion, by pronouncing what he calls the "upshot of the business," or, in other words, "the long and short of the matter."

Jack once made a journey to London, a great many years since, which has furnished him with topics of conversation ever since. He saw the old king on the terrace at Windsor, who stopped, and pointed him out to one of the princesses, being probably struck with Jack's truly yeoman-like appearance. This is a favourite anecdote with him, and has no doubt had a great effect in making him a most loyal subject ever since, in spite of taxes and poor's rates. He was also at Bartholomew-fair, where he had half the buttons cut off his coat; and a gang of pickpockets, attracted by his external show of gold and silver, made a regular attempt to hustle him as he was gazing at a show; but for once they found that they had caught a tartar, for Jack enacted as great wonders among the gang as Samson did among the Philistines. One of his neighbours, who had accompanied him to town, and was with him at the fair, brought back an account of his exploits, which raised the pride of the whole village; who considered their champion as having subdued all London, and eclipsed the achievements of Friar Tuck, or even the renowned Robin Hood himself.

Of late years the old fellow has begun to take the world easily; he works less, and indulges in greater leisure, his son having grown up, and succeeded to him both in the labours of the farm and the exploits of the green. Like all sons of distinguished men, however, his father's renown is a disadvantage to him, for he can never come up to public expectation. Though a fine, active fellow of three-and-twenty, and quite the "cock of the walk," yet the old people declare he is nothing like what Ready-Money Jack was at his time of life. The youngster himself acknowledges his inferiority, and has a wonderful opinion of the old man, who indeed taught him all his athletic accomplishments, and holds such a sway over him, that I am told, even to this day, he would have no hesitation to take him in hands, if he rebelled against paternal government.

The Squire holds Jack in very high esteem, and shows him

to all his visitors as a specimen of old English "heart of oak." He frequently calls at his house, and tastes some of his home-brewed, which is excellent. He made Jack a present of old Tusser's Hundred Points of good Husbandrie, which has furnished him with reading ever since, and is his text-book and manual in all agricultural and domestic concerns. He has made dog's ears at the most favourite passages, and knows many of the poetical maxims by heart.

Tibbets, though not a man to be daunted or fluttered by high acquaintances; and though he cherishes a sturdy independence of mind and manner, yet is evidently gratified by the attentions of the Squire, whom he has known from boyhood, and pronounces "a true gentleman every inch of him." He is also on excellent terms with Master Simon, who is a kind of privy councillor to the family; but his great favourite is the Oxonian, whom he taught to wrestle and play at quarter-staff when a boy, and considers the most promising young gentleman in the whole county.

BACHELORS

> The Bachelor most joyfully
> In pleasant plight doth pass his daies.
> Good fellowship and companie
> He doth maintain and kepe alwaies.
>
> EVANS' OLD BALLADS.

THERE is no character in the comedy of human life that is more difficult to play well than that of an old bachelor. When a single gentleman, therefore, arrives at that critical period when he begins to consider it an impertinent question to be asked his age, I would advise him to look well to his ways. This period, it is true, is much later with some men than with others; I have witnessed more than once the meeting of two wrinkled old lads of this kind, who had not seen each other for several years, and have been amused by the amicable exchange of compliments on each other's appearance that takes place on such occasions. There is always one invariable observation, "Why, bless my soul! you look younger than when last I saw you!" Whenever a man's friends begin to compliment him about looking young, he may be sure that they think he is growing old.

I am led to make these remarks by the conduct of Master Simon and the general, who have become great cronies. As the former is the younger by many years, he is regarded as quite a youthful gallant by the general, who moreover looks upon him as a man of great wit and prodigious acquirements. I have already hinted that Master Simon is a family beau, and considered rather a young fellow by all the elderly ladies of the connection, for an old bachelor, in an old family connection, is something like an actor in a regular dramatic corps, who seems " to flourish in immortal youth," and will continue to play the Romeos and Rangers for half a century together.

Master Simon, too, is a little of the chameleon, and takes a different hue with every different companion: he is very attentive and officious, and somewhat sentimental, with Lady Lillycraft; copies out little namby-pamby ditties and love-songs for her, and draws quivers, and doves, and darts, and Cupids, to be worked in the corners of her pocket-handkerchiefs. He indulges, however, in very considerable latitude with the other married ladies of the family; and has many sly pleasantries to whisper to them, that provoke an equivocal laugh and tap of the fan. But when he gets among your company, such as Frank Bracebridge, the Oxonian, and the general, he is apt to put on the mad wig, and to talk in a very bachelor-like strain about the sex.

In this he has been encouraged by the example of the general, whom he looks up to as a man who has seen the world. The general, in fact, tells shocking stories after dinner, when the ladies have retired, which he gives as some of the choice things that are served up at the Mulligatawney Club, a knot of boon companions in London. He also repeats the fat jokes of Major Pendergast, the wit of the club, and which, though the general can hardly repeat them for laughing, always make Mr. Bracebridge look grave, he having a great antipathy to an indecent jest. In a word, the general is a complete instance of the declension in gay life, by which a young man of pleasure is apt to cool down into an obscene old gentleman.

I saw him and Master Simon, an evening or two since, conversing with a buxom milkmaid in a meadow; and from their elbowing each other now and then, and the general's shaking his shoulders, blowing up his cheeks, and breaking out into a short fit of irrepressible laughter, I had no doubt they were playing the mischief with the girl.

As I looked at them through a hedge, I could not but think they would have made a tolerable group for a modern picture of Susannah and the two elders. It is true the girl seemed in no wise alarmed at the force of the enemy; and I question, had either of them been alone, whether she would not have been more than they would have ventured to encounter. Such veteran roisters are daring wags when together, and will put any female to the blush with their jokes; but they are as quiet as lambs when they fall singly into the clutches of a fine woman.

In spite of the general's years, he evidently is a little vain of his person, and ambitious of conquests. I have observed him on Sunday in church eyeing the country girls most suspiciously; and have seen him leer upon them with a downright amorous look, even when he has been gallanting Lady Lillycraft with great ceremony through the churchyard. The general, in fact, is a veteran in the service of Cupid rather than of Mars, having signalised himself in all the garrison towns and country quarters, and seen service in every ballroom of England. Not a celebrated beauty but he has laid siege to; and if his words may be taken in a matter wherein no man is apt to be over veracious, it is incredible what success he has had with the fair. At present he is like a worn-out warrior, retired from service; but who still cocks his beaver with a military air, and talks stoutly of fighting whenever he comes within the smell of gunpowder.

'I saw him and Master Simon conversing wit' a buxom milkmaid in a meadow.'

I have heard him speak his mind very freely over his bottle, about the folly of the captain in taking a wife; as he thinks a young soldier should care for nothing but his "bottle and kind landlady." But, in fact, he says, the service on the continent has had a sad effect upon the young men; they have been ruined by light wines and French quadrilles. "They've nothing," he says, "of the spirit of the old service. There are none of your six-bottle men left, that were the souls of a mess-dinner, and used to play the very deuce among the women."

As to a bachelor, the general affirms that he is a free and easy man, with no baggage to take care of but his portmanteau: but, as Major Pendergast says, a married man, with his wife

hanging on his arm, always puts him in mind of a chamber candlestick, with its extinguisher hitched to it. I should not mind all this if it were merely confined to the general; but I fear he will be the ruin of my friend, Master Simon, who already begins to echo his heresies, and to talk in the style of a gentleman that has seen life, and lived upon the town. Indeed, the general seems to have taken Master Simon in hand, and talks of showing him the lions when he comes to town, and of introducing him to a knot of choice spirits at the Mulligatawney Club; which, I understand, is composed of old nabobs, officers in the Company's employ, and other "men of Ind," that have seen service in the East, and returned home burnt out with curry and touched with the liver complaint. They have their regular club, where they eat Mulligatawney soup, smoke the hookah, talk about Tippoo Saib, Seringapatam, and tiger-hunting; and are tediously agreeable in each other's company.

A Literary Antiquary

Printed bookes he contemns, as a novelty of this latter age ; but a manuscript he pores on everlastingly : especially if the cover be all moth-eaten, and the dust make a parenthesis between every syllable.
                      Mico-Cosmographie. 1628.

THE Squire receives great sympathy and support in his antiquated humours, from the parson, of whom I made some mention on my former visit to the Hall, and who acts as a kind of family chaplain. He has been cherished by the Squire almost constantly since the time that they were fellow-students at Oxford ; for it is one of the peculiar advantages of these great universities, that they often link the poor scholar to the rich patron, by early and heartfelt ties, that last through life, without the usual humiliations of dependence and patronage. Under the fostering protection of the Squire, therefore, the little parson has pursued his studies in peace. Having lived almost entirely among books, and those, too, old books, he is quite ignorant of the world, and his mind is as antiquated as the garden at the Hall, where the flowers are all arranged in formal beds, and the yew-trees clipped into urns and peacocks.

His taste for literary antiquities was first imbibed in the Bodleian Library at Oxford; where, when a student, he passed many an hour foraging among the old manuscripts. He has since, at different times, visited most of the curious libraries in England, and has ransacked many of the cathedrals. With all his quaint and curious learning, he has nothing of arrogance or pedantry; but that unaffected earnestness and guileless simplicity which seem to belong to the literary antiquary.

He is a dark, mouldy little man, and rather dry in his manner; yet, on his favourite theme, he kindles up, and at times is even eloquent. No fox-hunter, recounting his last day's sport, could be more animated than I have seen the worthy parson, when relating his search after a curious document, which he had traced from library to library, until he fairly unearthed it in the dusty chapter-house of a cathedral. When, too, he describes some venerable manuscript, with its rich illuminations, its thick creamy vellum, its glossy ink, and the odour of the cloisters that seemed to exhale from it, he rivals the enthusiasm of a Parisian epicure, expatiating on the merits of a Perigord pie, or a *Pâté de Strasbourg*.

His brain seems absolutely haunted with love-sick dreams about gorgeous old works in "silk linings, triple gold bands, and tinted leather, locked up in wire cases, and secured from the vulgar hands of the mere reader;" and, to continue the happy expression of an ingenious writer, "dazzling one's eyes, like eastern beauties peering through their jealousies."

He has a great desire, however, to read such works in the old libraries and chapter-houses to which they belong; for he thinks a black-lettered volume reads best in one of those venerable chambers where the light struggles through dusty lancet windows and painted glass; and that it loses half its zest if taken away from the neighbourhood of the quaintly carved oaken book-case and Gothic reading-desk. At his suggestion, the squire has had the library furnished in this antique taste, and several of the windows glazed with painted glass, that they may throw a properly tempered light upon the pages of their favourite old authors.

Ｔhe parson, I am told, has been for some time meditating a commentary on Strutt, Brand, and Douce, in which he means to detect them in sundry dangerous errors in respect to popular games and superstitions ; a work to which the Squire looks forward with great interest. He is also a casual contributor to that long-established repository of national customs and antiquities, the Gentleman's Magazine, and is one of those that every now and then make an inquiry concerning some obsolete customs or rare legend ; nay, it is said that several of his communications have been at least six inches in length. He frequently receives parcels by coach from different parts of the kingdom, containing mouldy volumes and almost illegible manuscripts ; for it is singular what an active correspondence is kept up among literary antiquaries, and how soon the fame of any rare volume, or unique copy, just discovered among the rubbish of a library, is circulated among them. The parson is more busy than common just now, being a little flurried by an advertisement of a work, said to be preparing for the press, on the mythology of the middle ages. The little man has long been gathering together all the hobgoblin tales he could collect, illustrative of the superstitions of former times ; and he is in a complete fever lest this formidable rival should take the field before him.

Shortly after my arrival at the Hall, I called at the parsonage, in company with Mr. Bracebridge and the general. The parson had not been seen for several days, which was a matter of some surprise, as he was an almost daily visitor at the Hall. We found him in his study, a small, dusky chamber, lighted by a lattice window that looked into the churchyard, and was overshadowed by a yew-tree. His chair was surrounded by folios and quartos, piled upon the floor, and his table was covered with books and manuscripts. The cause of his seclusion was a work which he had recently received, and with which he had retired in rapture from the world, and shut himself up to enjoy a literary honeymoon undisturbed. Never did boarding-school girl devour the pages of a sentimental novel, or Don Quixote a chivalrous romance, with more

intense delight than did the little man banquet on the pages of this delicious work. It was Dibdin's Bibliographical Tour; a work calculated to have as intoxicating an effect on the imaginations of literary antiquaries as the adventures of the heroes of the Round Table on all true knights; or the tales of the early American voyagers on the ardent spirits of the age, filling them with dreams of Mexican and Peruvian mines, and of the golden realm of El Dorado.

The good parson had looked forward to this bibliographical expedition as of far greater importance that those to Africa, or the North Pole. With what eagerness had he seized upon the history of the enterprise! With what interest had he followed the redoubtable bibliographer and his graphical squire in their adventurous roamings among Norman castles and cathedrals, and French libraries, and German convents and universities; penetrating into the prison-houses of vellum manuscripts and exquisitely illuminated missals, and revealing their beauties to the world!

When the parson had finished a rapturous eulogy on this most curious and entertaining work, he drew forth from a little drawer a manuscript lately received from a correspondent, which perplexed him sadly. It was written in Norman-French in very ancient characters, and so faded and mouldered away as to be almost illegible. It was apparently an old Norman drinking song, that might have been brought over by one of William the Conqueror's carousing followers. The writing was just legible enough to keep a keen antiquity hunter on a doubtful chase; here and there he would be completely thrown out, and then there would be a few words so plainly written as to put him on the scent again. In this way he had been led on for a whole day, until he had found himself completely at fault.

The Squire endeavoured to assist him, but was equally baffled. The old general listened for some time to the discussion, and then asked the parson if he had read Captain Morris's or George Stephens's or Anacreon Moore's bacchanalian songs; on the other replying in the negative, "Oh, then," said the general, with a sagacious nod, "if you want a drinking song, I can furnish you with the latest collection—I did not know you had a turn for those kind of things; and I can lend you the Encyclopædia of Wit into the bargain. I never travel without them, they're excellent reading at an inn."

It would not be easy to describe the odd look of surprise and perplexity of the parson at this proposal; or the difficulty the Squire had in making the general comprehend, that though a jovial song of the present day was but a foolish sound in the ears of wisdom, and beneath the notice of a learned man, yet a trowl written by a tosspot several hundred years since was a matter worthy of the gravest research, and enough to set whole colleges by the ears.

I have since pondered much on this matter, and have figured to myself what may be the fate of our current literature, when retrieved piecemeal by future antiquaries, from among the rubbish of ages. What a Magnus Apollo, for instance, will Moore become among sober divines and dusty schoolmen! Even his festive and amatory songs, which are now the mere quickeners of our social moments, or the delights of our drawing-rooms, will then become matters of laborious research and painful collation. How many a grave professor will then waste his midnight oil, or worry his brain through a long morning, endeavouring to restore the pure text, or illustrate

the biographical hints of "Come tell me, says Rosa, as kissing and kissed;" and how many an arid old bookworm, like the worthy little parson, will give up in despair, after vainly striving to fill up some fatal hiatus in " Fanny of Timmol !"

Nor is it merely such exquisite authors as Moore that are doomed to consume the oil of future antiquaries. Many a poor scribbler, who is now apparently sent to oblivion by pastry-cooks and cheesemongers, will then rise again in fragments and flourish in learned immortality.

After all, thought I, time is not such an invariable destroyer as he is represented. If he pulls down, he likewise builds up; if he impoverishes one, he enriches another; his very dilapidations furnish matter for new works of controversy, and his rust is more precious than the most costly gilding. Under his plastic hand trifles rise into importance; the nonsense of one age becomes the wisdom of another; the levity of wit gravitates into the learning of the pedant, and an ancient farthing moulders into infinitely more value than a modern guinea.

THE FARM-HOUSE

> ———Love and hay
> Are thick sown, but come up full of thistles.
>
> BEAUMONT AND FLETCHER.

I WAS so much pleased with the anecdotes which were told me of Ready-Money Jack Tibbets, that I got Master Simon, a day or two since, to take me to his house. It was an old-fashioned farm-house, built of brick, with curiously twisted chimneys. It stood at a little distance from the road, with a southern exposure, looking upon a soft green slope of meadow. There was a small garden in front, with a row of beehives humming among beds of sweet herbs and flowers. Well-scoured milking tubs, with bright copper hoops, hung on the garden paling. Fruit trees were trained up against the cottage, and pots of flowers stood in the windows. A fat superannuated mastiff lay in the sunshine at the door; with a sleek cat sleeping peacefully across him.

Mr. Tibbets was from home at the time of our calling, but we were received with hearty and homely welcome by his wife

—a notable, motherly woman, and a complete pattern for wives, since, according to Master Simon's account, she never contradicts honest Jack, and yet manages to have her own way, and to control him in everything. She received us in the main room of the house, a kind of parlour or hall, with great brown beams of timber across it, which Mr. Tibbets is apt to point out with some exultation, observing that they don't put such timber in houses nowadays. The furniture was old-fashioned, strong, and highly polished; the walls were hung with coloured prints of the story of the Prodigal Son, who was represented in a red coat and leather breeches. Over the fireplace was a blunderbuss, and a hard-favoured likeness of Ready-Money Jack, taken when he was a young man, by the same artist that painted the tavern sign; his mother having taken a notion that the Tibbetses had as much right to have a gallery of family portraits as the folks at the Hall.

The good dame pressed us very much to take some refreshment, and tempted us with a variety of household dainties, so that we were glad to compound by tasting some of her home-made wines. While we were there, the son and heir-apparent came home; a good-looking young fellow, and something of a rustic beau. He took us over the premises, and showed us the whole establishment. An air of homely but substantial plenty prevailed throughout; everything was of the best materials, and in the best condition. Nothing was out of place, or ill made; and you saw everywhere the signs of a man that took care to have the worth of his money, and that paid as he went.

The farm-yard was well stocked; under a shed was a taxed cart, in trim order, in which Ready-Money Jack took his wife about the country. His well-fed horse neighed from the stable, and when led out into the yard, to use the words of young Jack, "he shone like a bottle;" for he said the old man made it a rule that everything about him should fare as well as he did himself.

I was pleased to see the pride which the young fellow seemed to have of his father. He gave us several particulars concerning his habits, which were pretty much to the effect of those I have already mentioned. He had never suffered an account to stand in his life, always providing the money before he purchased anything; and, if possible, paying in gold and silver. He had a great dislike to paper money, and seldom went without a considerable sum in gold about him. On my observing that it was a wonder he had never been waylaid and robbed, the young fellow smiled at the idea of any one venturing upon such an exploit, for I believe he thinks the old man would be a match for Robin Hood and all his gang.

I have noticed that Master Simon seldom goes into any house without having a word of private talk with some one or other of the family, being a kind of universal counsellor and confidant. We had not been long at the farm before the old dame got him into a corner of her parlour, where they had a long whispering conference together: in which I saw by his shrugs that there were some dubious matters discussed, and by his nods that he agreed with everything she said.

After we had come out, the young man accompanied us a little distance, and then, drawing Master Simon aside into a green lane, they walked and talked together for nearly half-an-hour. Master Simon, who has the usual propensity of confidants to blab everything to the next friend they meet with, let me know that there was a love affair in question; the young fellow having been smitten with the charms of Phœbe Wilkins, the pretty niece of the housekeeper at the Hall. Like most other love concerns, it had brought its troubles and perplexities. Dame Tibbets had long been on intimate gossiping terms with the housekeeper, who often visited the farm-house; but when the neighbours spoke to her of the likelihood of a match between her son and Phœbe Wilkins, "Marry come up!" she scouted the very idea. The girl had acted as lady's maid, and it was beneath the blood of the Tibbetses, who had lived on their own lands time out of mind, and owed reverence and thanks to nobody, to have the heir-apparent marry a servant!

These vapourings had faithfully been carried to the housekeeper's ear by one of the mutual go-between friends. The old housekeeper's blood, if not as ancient, was as quick as that of Dame Tibbets.

She had been accustomed to carry a high head at the Hall and among the villagers; and her faded brocade rustled with indignation at the slight cast upon her alliance by the wife of a petty farmer. She maintained that her niece had been a companion rather than a waiting-maid to the young ladies. "Thank heavens, she was not obliged to work for her living, and was as idle as any young lady in the land; and when somebody died, would receive something that would be worth the notice of some folks with all their ready money."

A bitter feud had thus taken place between the two worthy dames, and the young people were forbidden to think of one another. As to young Jack, he was too much in love to reason upon the matter; and being a little heady, and not standing in much awe of his mother, was ready to sacrifice the whole dignity of the Tibbetses to his passion. He had lately, however, had a violent quarrel with his mistress, in consequence of some coquetry on her part, and at present stood aloof. The politic mother was exerting all her ingenuity to widen this accidental breach; but, as is most commonly the case, the more she meddled with this perverse inclination of her son, the stronger it grew. In the meantime Old Ready-Money was kept completely in the dark; both parties were in awe and uncertainty as to what might be his way of taking the matter, and dreaded to awaken the sleeping lion. Between father and son, therefore, the worthy Mrs. Tibbets was full of business and at her wits' end. It is true that there was no great danger of honest Ready-Money's finding the thing out, if left to himself; for he was of a most unsuspicious temper, and by no means quick of apprehension; but there was daily risk of his attention being aroused by those cobwebs which his indefatigable wife was continually spinning about his nose. Such is the distracted state of politics in the domestic empire of Ready-Money Jack; which only shows the intrigues and internal dangers to which the best regulated governments are liable. In this perplexing situation of their affairs, both mother and son have applied to Master Simon for counsel; and, with all his experience in meddling with other people's concerns, he finds it an exceedingly difficult part to play, to agree with both parties, seeing that their opinions and wishes are so diametrically opposite.

HORSEMANSHIP

A coach was a strange monster in those days, and the sight of one put both horse and man into amazement. Some said it was a great crab-shell brought out of China, and some imagined it to be one of the Pagan temples in which the Cannibals adored the divell.

TAYLOR, THE WATER POET.

I HAVE made casual mention, more than once, of one of the squire's antiquated retainers, old Christy the huntsman. I find that his crabbed humour is a source of much entertainment among the young men of the family: the Oxonian, particularly, takes a mischievous pleasure now and then in slyly rubbing the old man against the grain, and then smoothing him down again; for the old fellow is as ready to bristle up his back as a porcupine. He rides a venerable hunter called Pepper, which is a counterpart of himself, a heady, cross-grained animal, that frets the flesh off its bones; bites, kicks, and plays all manner of villanous tricks. He is as tough, and nearly as old as his rider, who has ridden him time out of mind, and is, indeed, the only one that can do anything with him. Sometimes, however, they have a complete quarrel, and a dispute for mastery, and then, I am told, it is as good as a farce to see the heat they both get into, and the wrong-headed contest that ensues; for they are quite knowing in each other's ways and in the art of teasing and fretting each other. Notwithstanding these doughty brawls, however, there is nothing that nettles old Christy sooner than to question the merits of his horse; which he upholds as tenaciously as a faithful husband will vindicate the virtues of the termagant spouse that gives him a curtain lecture every night of his life.

The young men call old Christy their "professor of equitation," and in accounting for the appellation, they let me into some particulars of the Squire's mode of bringing up his children. There is an odd mixture of eccentricity and good sense in all the opinions of my worthy host. His mind is like modern Gothic, where plain brickwork is set off with pointed arches and plain tracery. Though the main groundwork of his opinions is correct, yet he has a thousand little notions, picked up from old books, which stand out whimsically on the surface of his mind.

Thus, in educating his boys, he chose Peachum, Markham, and such old English writers for his manuals. At an early age he took the lads out of their mother's hands, who was disposed, as mothers are apt to be, to make fine orderly children of them, that should keep out of sun and rain, and never soil their hands, nor tear their clothes.

In place of this, the Squire turned them loose, to run free and wild about the park, without heeding wind or weather. He was also particularly attentive in making them bold and expert horsemen; and these were the days when old Christy, the huntsman, enjoyed great importance, as the lads were put under his care to practice them at the leaping-bars, and to keep an eye upon them in the chase.

The Squire always objected to their using carriages of any kind, and is still a little tenacious on this point. He often rails against the universal use of carriages, and quotes the words of honest Nashe to that effect. "It was thought," says Nashe, in his Quaternio, "a kind of solecism, and to savour of effeminacy, for a young gentleman in the flourishing time of his age to creep into a coach, and to shroud himself from wind and weather; our great delight was to out-brave the blustering boreas upon a great horse; to arm and prepare ourselves to go with Mars and Bellona into the field was our sport and pastime; coaches and caroches we left unto them for whom they were first invented, for ladies and gentlemen, and decrepit age and impotent people."

The Squire insists that the English gentlemen have lost much of their hardiness and manhood since the introduction of carriages. "Compare," he will say, "the fine gentleman of former times, ever on horseback, booted and spurred, and travel-stained, but open, frank, manly, and chivalrous, with the fine gentleman of the present day, full of affectation and effeminacy, rolling along a turnpike in his voluptuous vehicle. The young men of those days were rendered brave, and lofty, and generous, in their notions, by almost living in their saddles, and having their foaming steeds 'like proud seas under them.' There is something," he adds, "in bestriding a fine horse, that makes a man feel more than mortal. He seems to have doubled his nature, and to have added to his own courage and sagacity the power, the speed, and stateliness of the superb animal on which he is mounted."

"It is a great delight," says old Nashe, "to see a young gentleman with his skill and cunning, by his voice, rod, and spur, better to manage and to command the great Bucephalus, than the strongest Milo, with all his strength; one while to see him make him tread, trot, and gallop the ring; and one after to see him make him gather up roundly; to bear his head steadily; to run a full career swiftly ; to stop a sudden lightly ; anon after to see him make him advance, to yorke, to go back and sidelong, to turn on either hand ; to gallop the gallop galliard ; to do the capriole, the chambetta, and dance the curvetty."

In conformity to these ideas, the Squire had them all on horseback at an early age, and made them ride, slap-dash, about the country, without flinching at hedge or ditch, or stone wall, to the imminent danger of their necks.

Even the fair Julia was partially included in this system ; and, under the instructions of old Christy, has become one of the best horsewomen in the county. The Squire says it is better than all the cosmetics and sweeteners of the breath that ever were invented. He extols the horsemanship of the ladies in former times, when Queen Elizabeth would scarcely suffer the rain to stop her accustomed ride. "And then think," he will say, "what nobler and sweeter beings it made them. What a difference must there be, both in mind and in body, between a joyous high-spirited dame of those days, glowing with health and exercise, freshened by every breeze that blows, seated loftily and gracefully on her saddle, with plume on head, and hawk on hand, and her descendant of the present day, the pale victim of routs and ball-rooms, sunk languidly in one corner of an enervating carriage."

The Squire's equestrian system has been attended with great success, for his sons, having passed through the whole course of instruction without breaking neck or limb, are now healthful, spirited, and active, and have the true Englishman's love for a horse. If their manliness and frankness are praised in their father's hearing, he quotes the old Persian maxim, and says, they have been taught "to ride, to shoot, and to speak the truth."

It is true the Oxonian has now and then practised the old gentleman's doctrines a little in the extreme. He is a gay youngster, rather fonder of his horse than his book, with a little dash of the dandy; though the ladies all declare that he

is "the flower of the flock." The first year that he was sent to Oxford he had a tutor appointed to overlook him, a dry chip of the university. When he returned home in the vacation, the Squire made many inquiries about how he liked his college, his studies, and his tutor. "Oh, as to my tutor, sir, I have parted with him some time since." "You have; and, pray, why so?" "Oh, sir, hunting was all the go at our college, and I was a little short of funds; so I discharged my tutor, and took a horse, you know." "Ah, I was not aware of that, Tom," said the Squire, mildly.

When Tom returned to college his allowance was doubled, that he might be enabled to keep both horse and tutor.

LOVE SYMPTOMS

> I will now begin to sigh, read poets, look pale, go neatly, and be most apparently in love.
>   MARSTON.

I SHOULD not be surprised if we should have another pair of turtles at the Hall, for Master Simon has informed me, in great confidence, that he suspects the general of some design upon the susceptible heart of Lady Lillycraft. I have, indeed, noticed a growing attention and courtesy in the veteran towards her ladyship; he softens very much in her company, sits by her at table, and entertains her with long stories about Seringapatam, and pleasant anecdotes of the Mulligatawney Club. I have even seen him present her with a full-blown rose from the hot-house, in a style of the most captivating gallantry, and it was accepted with great suavity and graciousness; for her ladyship delights in receiving the homage and attention of the sex.

Indeed, the general was one of the earliest admirers that dangled in her train during her short reign of beauty; and they flirted together for half a season in London, some thirty or forty years since. She reminded him lately, in the course of conversation about former days, of the time when he used to ride a white horse, and to canter so gallantly by the side of her carriage in Hyde Park; whereupon I have remarked that the veteran has regularly escorted her since, when she rides out on horseback; and I suspect he almost persuades himself that he makes as captivating an appearance as in his youthful days.

It would be an interesting and memorable circumstance in the chronicles of Cupid, if this spark of the tender passion, after lying dormant for such a length of time, should again be fanned into a flame from amidst the ashes of two burnt-out hearts. It would be an instance of perdurable fidelity, worthy of being placed beside those recorded in one of the Squire's favourite tomes, commemorating the constancy of the olden times; in which times, we are told, "men and wymmen coulde love togyders seven yeres, and no licours luste swere betwene them, and thenne was love, trouthe, and feythfulness; and lo in lyke wyse was used love in Kyng Arthurs dayes." *

Still, however, this may be nothing but a little venerable flirtation, the general being a veteran dangler, and the good lady habituated to these kind of attentions. Master Simon, on the other hand, thinks the general is looking about him with the wary eye of an old campaigner; and now that he is on the wane, is desirous of getting into warm winter quarters.

Much allowance, however, must be made for Master Simon's uneasiness on the subject, for he looks on Lady Lillycraft's house as one of the strongholds where he is lord of the ascendant; and, with all his admiration of the general, I much doubt whether he would like to see him lord of the lady and the establishment.

There are certain other symptoms, notwithstanding, that give an air of probability to Master Simon's intimations. Thus, for instance, I have observed that the general has been very

* Mort d'Arthur.

assiduous in his attentions to her ladyship's dogs, and has several times exposed his fingers to imminent jeopardy in attempting to pat Beauty on the head. It is to be hoped his advances to the mistress will be more favourably received, as all his overtures towards a caress are greeted by the pestilent little cur with a wary kindling of the eye, and a most venomous growl. He has, moreover, been very complaisant towards the lady's gentlewoman, the immaculate Mrs. Hannah, whom he

used to speak of in a way that I do not choose to mention. Whether she has the same suspicions with Master Simon or not, I cannot say; but she receives his civilities with no better grace than the implacable Beauty; unscrewing her mouth into a most acid smile, and looking as though she could bite a piece out of him. In short, the poor general seems to have as formidable foes to contend with as a hero of ancient fairy tale, who had to fight his way to his enchanted princess through ferocious monsters of every kind, and to encounter the brimstone terrors of some fiery dragon.

There is still another circumstance which inclines me to give very considerable credit to Master Simon's suspicions. Lady Lillycraft is very fond of quoting poetry, and the conversation often turns upon it, on which occasions the general is thrown completely out. It happened the other day that Spenser's Fairy Queen was the theme for the great part of the morning, and the poor general sat perfectly silent. I found him not long after in the library with spectacles on nose, a book in his hand, and fast asleep. On my approach he awoke, slipped the spectacles into his pocket, and began to read very attentively. After a little while he put a paper in the place, and laid the volume aside, which I perceived was the Fairy Queen. I have had the curiosity to watch how he got on in his poetical studies; but though I have repeatedly seen him with the book in his hand, yet I find the paper has not advanced above three or four pages; the general being extremely apt to fall asleep when he reads.

FALCONRY

> Ne is there hawk which mantleth on her perch,
> Whether high tow'ring or accousting low,
> But I the measure of her flight doe search,
> And all her prey and all her diet know.   SPENSER.

THERE are several grand sources of lamentation furnished to the worthy Squire by the improvement of society, and the grievous advancement of knowledge; among which there is none, I believe, that causes him more frequent regret than the unfortunate invention of gunpowder. To this he continually traces the decay of some favourite custom, and, indeed, the general downfall of all chivalrous and romantic usages. "English soldiers," he says, "have never been the men they were in the days of the cross-bow and the long-bow; when they depended upon the strength of the arm, and the English archer could draw a cloth-yard shaft to the head. These were the times when, at the battles of Cressy, Poictiers, and Agincourt, the French chivalry was completely destroyed by the bowmen of England. The yeomanry, too, have never been what they were, when, in times of peace, they were constantly exercised with the bow, and archery was a favourite holiday pastime."

Among the other evils which have followed in the train of this fatal invention of gunpowder, the Squire classes the total decline of the noble art of falconry. "Shooting," he says, "is a skulking, treacherous, solitary sport in comparison; but hawking was a gallant, open, sunshiny recreation; it was the generous sport of hunting carried into the skies."

"It was, moreover," he says, "according to Braithewaite, the stately amusement of high and mounting spirits; for, as the old Welsh proverb affirms, in those times 'You might know a gentleman by his hawk, horse, and greyhound.' Indeed, a cavalier was seldom seen abroad without his hawk on his fist; and even a lady of rank did not think herself completely equipped, in riding forth, unless she had her tassel-gentel held by jesses on her delicate hand. It was thought in those excellent days, according to an old writer, 'quite sufficient for noblemen to winde their horn, and to carry their hawke fair; and leave study and learning to the children of mean people.'"

Knowing the good Squire's hobby, therefore, I have not been surprised at finding that, among the various recreations of former times which he has endeavoured to revive in the little world in which he rules, he has bestowed great attention on the noble art of falconry. In this he of course has been seconded by his indefatigable coadjutor, Master Simon: and even the parson has thrown considerable light on their labours, by various hints on the subject, which he has met with in old English works. As to the precious work of that famous dame, Julianna Barnes; the Gentleman's Academie, by Markham; and the other well-known treatises that were the manuals of ancient sportsmen, they have them at their fingers' ends: but they have more especially studied some old tapestry in the house, whereon is represented a party of cavaliers and stately dames, with doublets, caps, and flaunting feathers, mounted on horse, with attendants on foot, all in animated pursuit of the game.

The Squire has discountenanced the killing of any hawks in his neighbourhood, but gives a liberal bounty for all that are brought him alive; so that the Hall is well stocked with all kinds of birds of prey. On these he and Master Simon have exhausted their patience and ingenuity, endeavouring to "reclaim" them, as it is termed, and to train them up for the sport; but they have met with continual checks and disappointments. Their feathered school has turned out the most intractable and graceless scholars; nor is it the least of their trouble to drill the retainers who were to act as ushers under them, and to take immediate charge of these refractory birds. Old Christy and the gamekeeper both, for a time, set their faces against the whole plan of education; Christy having been nettled at hearing what he terms a wild-goose chase put on a par with a fox-hunt; and the gamekeeper having always been accustomed to look upon hawks as arrant poachers, which it was his duty to shoot down, and nail, *in terrorem*, against the outhouses.

Christy has at length taken the matter in hand, but has done still more mischief by his intermeddling. He is as positive and wrong-headed about this as he is about hunting. Master Simon has continual disputes with him as to feeding and training the hawks. He reads to him long passages from the old authors I have mentioned; but Christy, who cannot read, has a sovereign contempt for all book-knowledge, and persists in treating the hawks according to his own notions, which are drawn from his experience, in younger days, in rearing of game cocks.

The consequence is, that, between these jarring systems, the poor birds have had a most trying and unhappy time of it. Many have fallen victims to Christy's feeding and Master Simon's physicking; for the latter has gone to work *secundum artem*, and has given them all the vomitings and scourings laid down in the books; never were poor hawks so fed and physicked before. Others have been lost by being but half "reclaimed,"

or tamed; for on being taken into the field they have "raked" after the game quite out of hearing of the call, and never returned to school.

All these disappointments had been petty, yet sore grievances to the Squire, and had made him to despond about success. He has lately, however, been made happy by the receipt of a fine Welsh falcon, which Master Simon terms a stately highflyer. It is a present from the Squire's friend, Sir Watkyn Williams Wynn; and is, no doubt, a descendant of some ancient line of Welsh princes of the air, that have long lorded it over their kingdom of clouds, from Wynnstay to the very summit of Snowdon, or the brow of Penmanmawr. Ever since the Squire received this invaluable present, he has been as impatient to sally forth and make proof of it, as was Don Quixote to assay his suit of armour. There have been some demurs as to whether the bird was in proper health and training; but these have been overruled by the vehement desire to play with a new toy; and it has been determined, right or wrong, in season or out of season, to have a day's sport in hawking to-morrow.

The Hall, as usual, whenever the Squire is about to make some new sally on his hobby, is all agog with the thing. Miss Templeton, who is brought up in reverence for all her guardian's humours, has proposed to be of the party, and Lady Lillycraft has talked also of riding out to the scene of action and looking on. This has gratified the old gentleman extremely; he hails it as an auspicious omen of the revival of falconry, and does not despair but the time will come when it will be again the pride of a fine lady to carry about a noble falcon in preference to a parrot or a lapdog.

I have amused myself with the bustling preparations of that busy spirit, Master Simon, and the continual thwartings he receives from that genuine son of a pepper-box, old Christy.

They have had half a dozen consultations about how the hawk is to be prepared for the morning's sport. Old Nimrod, as usual, has always got in a pet, upon which Master Simon has invariably given up the point, observing in a good-humoured tone, "Well, well, have it your own way, Christy; only don't put yourself in a passion;" a reply which always nettles the old man ten times more than ever.

HAWKING

> The soaring hawk, from fist that flies,
>   Her falconer doth constrain
> Sometimes to range the ground about
>   To find her out again ;
> And if by sight, or sound of bell,
>   His falcon he may see,
> Wo ho ! he cries with cheerful voice—
>   The gladdest man is he.
>
> *Handefull of Pleasant Delites.*

AT an early hour this morning the Hall was in a bustle, preparing for the sport of the day. I heard Master Simon whistling and singing under my window at sunrise, as he was preparing the jesses for the hawk's legs, and could distinguish now and then a stanza of one of his favourite old ditties :

> " In peascod time, when hound to horn
>   Gives note that buck be kill'd ;
> And little boy with pipe of corn
>   Is tending sheep a-field." etc.

A hearty breakfast, well flanked by cold meats, was served up in the great hall. The whole garrison of retainers and hangers-on were in motion, reinforced by volunteer idlers from the village. The horses were led up and down before the door; everybody had something to say and something to do, and hurried hither and thither; there was a direful yelping of dogs; some that were to accompany us being eager to set off, and others that were to stay at home being whipped back to their kennels. In short, for once, the good Squire's mansion might have been taken as a good specimen of one of the rantipole establishments of the good old feudal times.

Breakfast being finished, the chivalry of the Hall prepared to take the field. The fair Julia was of the party, in a hunting-dress, with a light plume of feathers in her riding-hat. As she mounted her favourite Galloway, I remarked, with pleasure, that old Christy forgot his usual crustiness, and hastened to adjust her saddle and bridle. He touched his cap as she smiled on him and thanked him; and then, looking round at the other attendants, gave a knowing nod of his head, in which I read pride and exultation at the charming appearance of his pupil.

Lady Lillycraft had likewise determined to witness the sport. She was dressed in her broad white beaver, tied under the chin, and a riding-habit of the last century. She rode her sleek, ambling pony, whose motion was as easy as a rocking-chair; and was gallantly escorted by the general, who looked not unlike one of the doughty heroes in the old prints of the battle of Blenheim. The parson, likewise, accompanied her on the other side; for this was a learned amusement in which he took great interest; and, indeed, had given much counsel, from his knowledge of old customs.

At length everything was arranged, and off we set from the Hall. The exercise on horseback puts one in fine spirits; and the scene was gay and animating. The young men of the family accompanied Miss Templeton. She sat lightly and gracefully in her saddle, her plumes dancing and waving in the air; and the group had a charming effect as they appeared and disappeared among the trees, cantering along with the bounding animation of youth. The Squire and Master Simon rode

HAWKING

together, accompanied by old Christy mounted on Pepper. The latter bore the hawk on his fist, as he insisted the bird was most accustomed to him. There was a rabble rout on foot, composed of retainers from the Hall, and some idlers from the village, with two or three spaniels for the purpose of starting the game.

A kind of *corps de reserve* came on quietly in the rear, composed of Lady Lillycraft, General Harbottle, the parson, and a fat footman. Her ladyship ambled gently along on her pony, while the general, mounted on a tall hunter, looked down upon her with an air of the most protecting gallantry.

For my part, being no sportsman, I kept with this last party, or rather lagged behind, that I might take in the whole picture; and the parson occasionally slackened his pace and jogged on in company with me.

The sport led us at some distance from the Hall, in a soft meadow reeking with the moist verdure of spring. A little

river ran through it, bordered by willows, which had put forth their tender early foliage. The sportsmen were in quest of herons, which were said to keep about this stream.

There was some disputing already among the leaders of the sport. The Squire, Master Simon, and old Christy, came every now and then to a pause, to consult together, like the field officers in an army; and I saw, by certain motions of the head, that Christy was as positive as any old wrong-headed German commander.

As we were prancing up this quiet meadow every sound we made was answered by a distinct echo, from the sunny wall of an old building that lay on the opposite margin of the stream; and I paused to listen to the "spirit of a sound," which seems to love such quiet and beautiful places. The parson informed me that this was the ruin of an ancient grange, and was supposed by the country people to be haunted by a dobbie, a kind of rural sprite, something like Robin Goodfellow. They often fancied the echo to be the voice of the dobbie answering them, and were rather shy of disturbing it after dark. He added, that the Squire was very careful of this ruin, on account of the superstition connected with it. As I considered this local habitation of an "airy nothing," I called to mind the fine description of an echo in Webster's Duchess of Malfy:

> ———"Yond side o' th' river lies a wall,
> Piece of a cloister, which in my opinion
> Gives the best echo that you have ever heard:
> So plain in the distinction of our words
> That many have supposed it a spirit
> That answers."

The parson went on to comment on a pleasing and fanciful appellation which the Jews of old gave to the echo, which they called Bath-Kool, that is to say, "the daughter of the voice;" they considered it an oracle, supplying in the second temple the want of the Urim and Thummim, with which the first was honoured.* The little man was just entering very largely and learnedly upon the subject, when we were startled by a prodigious bawling, shouting, and yelping. A flight of crows, alarmed by the approach of our forces, had suddenly arisen from a meadow; a cry was put up by the rabble rout on foot

* Bekker's *Monde Enchanté*.

"Now, Christy! now is your time, Christy!" The Squire and Master Simon, who were beating up the river banks in quest of a heron, called out eagerly to Christy to keep quiet; the old man, vexed and bewildered by the confusion of voices, completely lost his head: in his flurry he slipped off the hood, cast off the falcon, and away flew the crows, and away soared the hawk.

I had paused on a rising ground, close to Lady Lillycraft and her escort, from whence I had a good view of the sport. I was pleased with the appearance of the party in the meadow, riding along in the direction that the bird flew; their bright beaming faces turned up to the bright skies as they watched the game; the attendants on foot scampering along, looking up, and calling out, and the dogs bounding and yelping with clamorous sympathy.

The hawk had singled out a quarry from among the carrion crew. It was curious to see the efforts of the two birds to get above each other; one to make the fatal swoop, the other to avoid it. Now they crossed athwart a bright feathery cloud, and now they were against the clear blue sky. I confess, being no sportsman, I was more interested for the poor bird that was striving for its life, than for the hawk that was playing the part of a mercenary soldier. At length the hawk got the upper hand, and made a rushing stoop at her quarry, but the latter made as sudden a surge downwards, and slanting up again evaded the blow, screaming and making the best of his way for a dry tree on the brow of a neighbouring hill; while the hawk, disappointed of her blow, soared up again into the air, and appeared to be "raking" off. It was in vain old Christy called and whistled, and endeavoured to lure her down; she paid no regard to him; and, indeed, his calls were drowned in the shouts and yelps of the army of militia that had followed him into the field.

Just then an exclamation from Lady Lillycraft made me turn my head. I beheld a complete confusion among the

sportsmen in the little vale below us. They were galloping and running towards the edge of a bank; and I was shocked to see Miss Templeton's horse galloping at large without his rider. I rode to the place to which the others were hurrying, and when I reached the bank, which almost overhung the stream, I saw at the foot of it the fair Julia, pale, bleeding, and apparently lifeless, supported in the arms of her frantic lover.

In galloping heedlessly along, with her eyes turned upward, she had unwarily approached too near the bank; it had given way with her, and she and her horse had been precipitated to the pebbled margin of the river.

I never saw greater consternation. The captain was distracted; Lady Lillycraft fainting; the Squire in dismay; and Master Simon at his wits' end. The beautiful creature at length showed signs of returning life; she opened her eyes; looked around her upon the anxious group, and comprehending in a moment the nature of the scene, gave a sweet smile, and putting her hand in her lover's, exclaimed feebly, " I am not much hurt, Guy!" I could have taken her to my heart for that single exclamation.

It was found, indeed, that she had escaped, almost miraculously, with a contusion of the head, a sprained ankle, and some slight bruises. After her wound was staunched, she was taken to a neighbouring cottage until a carriage could be summoned to convey her home; and when this had arrived the cavalcade, which had issued forth so gaily on this enterprise, returned slowly and pensively to the Hall.

I had been charmed by the generous spirit shown by this young creature, who, amidst pain and danger, had been anxious only to relieve the distress of those around her. I was gratified, therefore, by the universal concern displayed by the domestics on our return. They came crowding down the avenue, each eager to render assistance. The butler stood ready with some curiously delicate cordial; the old housekeeper was provided with half a dozen nostrums, prepared by her own hands, according to the family receipt book; while her niece, the melting Phœbe, having no other way of assisting, stood wringing her hands and weeping aloud.

The most material effect that is likely to follow this accident is a postponement of the nuptials, which were close at hand. Though I commiserate the impatience of the captain on that account, yet I shall not otherwise be sorry at the delay, as it will give me a better opportunity of studying the characters here assembled, with which I grow more and more entertained.

I cannot but perceive that the worthy Squire is quite disconcerted at the unlucky result of his hawking experiment, and this unfortunate illustration of his eulogy on female equitation. Old Christy, too, is very waspish, having been sorely twitted by Master Simon for having let his hawk fly at carrion. As to the falcon, in the confusion occasioned by the fair Julia's disaster the bird was totally forgotten. I make no doubt she has made the best of her way back to the hospitable Hall of Sir Watkyn Williams Wynn; and may very possibly, at this present writing, be pluming her wings among the breezy bowers of Wynnstay.

FORTUNE-TELLING

Each city, each town, and every village
Affords us either an alms or pillage.
And if the weather be cold and raw,
Then in a barn we tumble on straw.
If warm and fair, by yea-cock and nay-cock,
The fields will afford us a hedge or a hay-cock.
Merry Beggars.

As I was walking one evening with the Oxonian, Master Simon, and the general, in a meadow not far from the village, we heard the sound of a fiddle rudely played, and looking in the direction from whence it came, we saw a thread of smoke curling up from among the trees. The sound of music is always attractive; for, wherever there is music, there is good-humour or goodwill. We passed along a footpath, and had a peep, through a break in the hedge, at the musician and his party, when the Oxonian gave us a wink, and told us that if we would follow him we should have some sport.

It proved to be a gipsy encampment, consisting of three or

four little cabins, or tents, made of blankets and sailcloth, spread over hoops that were stuck in the ground. It was on one side of a green lane, close under a hawthorn hedge, with a broad beech-tree spreading above it. A small rill tinkled along close by, through the fresh sward, that looked like a carpet.

A tea-kettle was hanging by a crooked piece of iron, over a fire made from dry sticks and leaves, and two old gipsies, in red cloaks, sat crouched on the grass, gossiping over their evening cup of tea ; for these creatures, though they live in the open air, have their ideas of fireside comforts. There were two or three children sleeping on the straw with which the tents were littered ; a couple of donkeys were grazing in the lane, and a thievish-looking dog was lying before the fire. Some of the younger gipsies were dancing to the music of a fiddle, played by a tall, slender stripling, in an old frock coat, with a peacock's feather stuck in his hatband.

As we approached, a gipsy girl, with a pair of fine roguish eyes, came up, and, as usual, offered to tell our fortunes. I

could not but admire a certain degree of slattern elegance about the baggage. Her long black silken hair was curiously plaited in numerous small braids, and negligently put up in a picturesque style that a painter might have been proud to have devised. Her dress was of a figured chintz, rather ragged, and not over clean, but of a variety of most harmonious and agreeable colours ; for these beings have a singularly fine eye for colours. Her straw hat was in her hand, and a red cloak thrown over one arm. The Oxonian offered at once to have his fortune told, and the girl began with the usual volubility of her race ; but he drew her on one side near the hedge, as he said he had no idea of having his secrets overheard. I saw he was talking to her instead of she to him, and by his glancing towards us now and then, that he was giving the baggage some private hints. When they returned to us he assumed a very serious air. "Zounds!" said he, "it's very astonishing how these creatures come by their knowledge; this girl has told me some things that I thought no one knew but myself!"

The girl now assailed the general; "Come, your honour," said she, "I see by your face you're a lucky man; but you're not happy in your mind; you're not, indeed, sir; but have a good heart, and give me a good piece of silver, and I'll tell you a nice fortune." The general had received all her approaches with a banter, and had suffered her to get hold of his hand; but at the mention of the piece of silver, he hemmed, looked grave, and turning to us, asked if we had not better continue our walk. "Come, my master," said the girl archly, "you'd not be in such a hurry if you knew  all that I could tell you about a fair lady that has a notion for you. Come, sir, old love burns strong; there's many a one comes to see weddings that go away brides themselves!" Here the girl whispered something in a low voice, at which the general coloured up, was a little fluttered, and suffered himself to be drawn aside under the hedge, where he appeared to listen to her with great earnestness, and at the end paid her half-a-crown with the air of a man that has got the worth of his money.

The girl next made her attack upon Master Simon, who, however, was too old a bird to be caught, knowing that it would end in an attack upon his purse, about which he is a little sensitive. As he has a great notion, however, of being considered a roister, he chucked her under the chin, played her off with rather broad jokes, and put on something of the rake-helly air, that we see now and then assumed on the stage by the sad-boy gentlemen of the old school. "Ah, your honour," said the girl, with a malicious leer, "you were not in such a tantrum last year when I told you about the widow, you know who; but if you had taken a friend's advice, you'd never have come away from Doncaster races with a flea in your ear!"

There was a secret sting in this speech that seemed quite to disconcert Master Simon. He jerked away his hand in a pet, smacked his whip, whistled to his dogs, and intimated that it was high time to go home. The girl, however, was determined not to lose her harvest. She now turned upon me, and, as I have a weakness of spirit where there is a pretty face concerned, she soon wheedled me out of my money, and in return read me a fortune which, if it prove true, and I am determined to believe it, will make me one of the luckiest men in the chronicles of Cupid.

I saw that the Oxonian was at the bottom of all this oracular mystery, and was disposed to amuse himself with the general, whose tender approaches to the widow have attracted the notice of the wag. I was a little curious, however, to know the meaning of the dark hints which had so suddenly disconcerted Master Simon: and took occasion to fall in the rear with the Oxonian on our way home, when he laughed heartily at my questions, and gave me ample information on the subject.

The truth of the matter is, that Master Simon has met with

a sad rebuff since my Christmas visit to the Hall. He used at that time to be joked about a widow, a fine dashing woman, as he privately informed me. I had supposed the pleasure he betrayed on these occasions resulted from the usual fondness of old bachelors for being teased about getting married, and about flirting, and being fickle and false-hearted. I am assured, however, that Master Simon had really persuaded himself the widow had a kindness for him; in consequence of which he had been at some extraordinary expense in new clothes, and had actually got Frank Bracebridge to order him a coat from Stultz. He began to throw out hints about the importance of a man's settling himself in life before he grew old; he would look grave whenever the widow and matrimony were mentioned in the same sentence; and privately asked the opinion of the Squire and parson about the prudence of marrying a widow with a rich jointure, but who had several children.

An important member of a great family connection cannot harp much upon the theme of matrimony without its taking wind; and it soon got buzzed about that Mr. Simon Bracebridge was actually gone to Doncaster races, with a new horse, but that he meant to return in a curricle with a lady by his side. Master Simon, did, indeed, go to the races, and that with a new horse; and the dashing widow did make her appearance in her curricle; but it was unfortunately driven by a strapping young Irish dragoon, with whom even Master Simon's self-complacency would not allow him to enter into competition, and to whom she was married shortly after.

It was a matter of sore chagrin to Master Simon for several months, having never before been fully committed. The dullest head in the family had a joke upon him; and there is no one that likes less to be bantered than an absolute joker. He took refuge for a time at Lady Lillycraft's, until the matter should blow over; and occupied himself by looking over her accounts, regulating the village choir, and inculcating loyalty into a pet bullfinch by teaching him to whistle "God save the King." He has now pretty nearly recovered from the mortification; holds up his head, and laughs as much as any one; again affects to pity married men, and is particularly facetious about widows, when Lady Lillycraft is not by. His only time of trial is when the general gets hold of him, who is infinitely heavy and persevering in his waggery, and will interweave a dull joke through the various topics of a whole dinner-time. Master Simon often parries these attacks by a stanza from his old work of "Cupid's Solicitor for Love:"

> "'Tis in vain to woo a widow over long,
>   In once or twice her mind you may perceive;
> Widows are subtle, be they old or young,
>   And by their wiles young men they will deceive."

LOVE-CHARMS

———Come, do not weep, my girl,
Forget him, pretty pensiveness; there will
Come others, every day, as good as he.
SIR J. SUCKLING.

THE approach of a wedding in a family is always an event of great importance, but particularly so in a household like this, in a retired part of the country. Master Simon, who is a pervading spirit, and, through means of the butler and housekeeper, knows everything that goes forward, tells me that the maid-servants are continually trying their fortunes, and that the servants' hall has of late been quite a scene of incantation.

It is amusing to notice how the oddities of the head of a family flow down through all the branches. The Squire, in the indulgence of his love of everything that smacks of old times, has held so many grave conversations with the parson at table, about popular superstitions and traditional rites, that they have been carried from the parlour to the kitchen by the listening domestics, and, being apparently sanctioned by such high authorities, the whole house has become infected by them.

The servants are all versed in the common modes of trying luck, and the charms to ensure constancy. They read their fortunes by drawing strokes in the ashes, or by repeating a form of words, and looking in a pail of water. St. Mark's Eve, I am told, was a busy time with them; being an appointed night for certain mystic ceremonies. Several of them sowed hemp seed, to be reaped by their true lovers; and they even ventured upon the solemn and fearful preparation of the dumb-cake. This must be done fasting and in silence. The ingredients are handed down in traditional form;—" An egg-shell full of salt, an egg-shell full of malt, and an egg-shell full of barley meal." When the cake is ready, it is put on a pan over the fire, and the future husband will appear, turn the cake, and retire; but if a word is spoken, or a fast is broken, during this awful ceremony, there is no knowing what horrible consequence would ensue!

The experiments in the present instance came to no result; they that sowed the hemp-seed forgot the magic rhyme that they were to pronounce, so the true lover never appeared; and as to the dumb-cake, what between the awful stillness they had to keep, and the awfulness of the midnight hour, their hearts failed them when they had put the cake in the pan, so that, on the striking of the great house-clock in the servants' hall, they were seized with a sudden panic, and ran out of the room, to which they did not return until morning, when they found the mystic cake burnt to a cinder.

The most persevering at these spells, however, is Phœbe Wilkins, the housekeeper's niece. As she is a kind of privileged personage, and rather idle, she has more time to occupy herself with these matters. She has always had her head full of love and matrimony, she knows the dreaming book by heart, and is quite an oracle among the little girls of the family, who always come to her to interpret their dreams in the mornings.

During the present gaiety of the house, however, the poor girl has worn a face full of trouble; and, to use the housekeeper's words, "has fallen into a sad hystericky way lately." It seems that she was born and brought up in the village, where her father was parish-clerk, and she was an early playmate and sweetheart of young Jack Tibbets. Since she has come to live at the Hall, however, her head has been a little turned. Being very pretty, and naturally genteel, she has been much noticed and indulged: and being the housekeeper's niece, she has held an equivocal station between a servant and a companion. She has learned something of fashions and notions among the young ladies, which have effected quite a metamorphosis; insomuch that her finery at church on Sundays has given mortal offence to her former intimates in the village. This has occasioned the misrepresentations which have awakened the implacable family pride of Dame Tibbets. But what is worse, Phœbe, having a spice of coquetry in her disposition, showed it on one or two occasions to her lover, which produced a downright quarrel; and Jack, being very proud and fiery, has absolutely turned his back upon her for several successive Sundays.

The poor girl is full of sorrow and repentance, and would fain make up with her lover; but he feels his security and stands aloof. In this he is doubtless encouraged by his mother, who is continually reminding him of what he owes to his family; for this same family pride seems doomed to be the eternal bane of lovers.

As I hate to see a pretty face in trouble, I have felt quite concerned for the luckless Phœbe, ever since I heard her story. It is a sad thing to be thwarted in love at any time, but particularly so at this tender season of the year, when every living thing, even to the very butterfly, is sporting with its mate ; and the green fields and the budding groves, and the singing of the birds, and the sweet smell of the flowers, are enough to turn the head of a love-sick girl. I am told that

the coolness of young Ready-Money lies heavy at poor Phœbe's heart. Instead of singing about the house as formerly, she goes about pale and sighing, and is apt to break into tears when her companions are full of merriment.

Mrs. Hannah, the vestal gentlewoman of my Lady Lillycraft, has had long talks and walks with Phœbe, up and down the avenue, of an evening ; and has endeavoured to squeeze some of her own verjuice into the other's milky nature. She speaks with contempt and abhorrence of the whole sex, and advises Phœbe to despise all the men as heartily as she does. But Phœbe's loving temper is not to be curdled ; she has no such thing as hatred or contempt for mankind in her whole composition. She has all the simple fondness of heart of poor, weak, loving woman ; and her only thoughts at present are, how to conciliate and reclaim her wayward swain. The spells and love-charms, which are matters of sport to the other domestics, are serious concerns with this love-stricken damsel. She is continually trying her fortune in a variety of ways. I am told that she has absolutely fasted for six Wednesdays and three Fridays successively, having understood that it was a sovereign charm to ensure being married to one's liking within the year. She carries about, also, a lock of her sweetheart's hair, and a riband he once gave her, being a mode of producing constancy in her lover. She even went so far as

to try her fortune by the moon, which has always had much to do with lovers' dreams and fancies. For this purpose she went out in the night of the full moon, knelt on a stone in the meadow, and repeated the old traditional rhyme:

> "All hail to thee, moon, all hail to thee :
> I pray thee, good moon, now show to me
> The youth who my future husband shall be."

When she came back to the house, she was faint and pale, and went immediately to bed. The next morning she told the porter's wife that she had seen some one close by the hedge in the meadow, which she was sure was young Tibbets; at any rate, she had dreamt of him all night; both of which, the old dame assured her, were most happy signs. It has since turned out that the person in the meadow was old Christy, the huntsman, who was walking his nightly rounds with the great staghound; so that Phœbe's faith in the charm is completely shaken.

A BACHELOR'S CONFESSIONS.

I'll have a private, pensive single life.
The Collier of Croydon.

I WAS sitting in my room a morning or two since, reading, when some one tapped at the door, and Master Simon entered. He had an unusually fresh appearance; he had put on a bright green riding-coat, with a bunch of violets in the button-hole, and had the air of an old bachelor trying to rejuvenate himself. He had not, however, his usual briskness and vivacity, but loitered about the room with somewhat of absence of manner, humming the old song—"Go, lovely rose, tell her that wastes her time and me;" and then, leaning against the window and looking upon the landscape, he uttered a very audible sigh. As I had not been accustomed to see Master Simon in a pensive mood, I thought there might be some vexation preying on his mind, and I endeavoured to introduce a cheerful strain of conversation; but he was not in the vein to follow it up, and proposed that we should take a walk.

It was a beautiful morning, of that soft vernal temperature that seems to thaw all the frost out of one's blood, and to set all nature in a ferment. The very fishes felt its influence; the cautious trout ventured out of his dark hole to seek his mate, the roach and the dace rose up to the surface of the brook to bask in the sunshine, and the amorous frog piped from among the rushes. If ever an oyster can really fall in love, as has been said or sung, it must be on such a morning.

The weather certainly had its effect even upon Master Simon, for he seemed obstinately bent upon the pensive mood. Instead of stepping briskly along, smacking his dog-whip, whistling quaint ditties, or telling sporting anecdotes, he leaned on my arm, and talked about the approaching nuptials; from whence he made several digressions upon the character of womankind, touched a little upon the tender passion, and made sundry very excellent, through rather trite, observations upon disappointments in love. It was evident that he had something on his mind which he wished to impart, but felt awkward in approaching it. I was curious to see to what this strain would lead; but I was determined not to assist him. Indeed, I mischievously pretended to turn the conversation, and talked of his usual topics, dogs, horses, and hunting; but he was very brief in his replies, and invariably got back, by hook or by crook, into the sentimental vein.

At length we came to a clump of trees that overhung a whispering brook, with a rustic bench at their feet. The trees were grievously scored with letters and devices, which had grown out of all shape and size by the growth of the bark; and it appeared that this grove had served as a kind of register of the family loves from time immemorial. Here Master Simon made a pause, pulled up a tuft of flowers, threw them one by one into the water, and at length, turning somewhat abruptly upon me, asked me if ever I had been in love. I confess the question startled me a little, as I am not over fond of making confessions of my amorous follies; and above all, should never dream of choosing my friend Master Simon for a

'Here Master Simon made a pause, pulled up a tuft of flowers, and threw them one by one into the water.'

confidant. He did not wait, however, for a reply; the inquiry was merely a prelude to a confession on his own part, and after several circumlocutions and whimsical preambles, he fairly disburthened himself of a very tolerable story of his having been crossed in love.

The reader will, very probably, suppose that it related to the gay widow who jilted him not long since at Doncaster races;—no such thing. It was about a sentimental passion that he once had for a most beautiful young lady, who wrote poetry and played on the harp. He used to serenade her; and indeed he described several tender and gallant scenes, in which he was evidently picturing himself in his mind's eye as some elegant hero of romance, though, unfortunately for the tale, I only saw him as he stood before me, a dapper little old bachelor, with a face like an apple that has dried with the bloom on it.

What were the particulars of this tender tale I have already forgotten; indeed I listened to it with a heart like a very pebble stone, having hard work to repress a smile while Master Simon was putting on the amorous swain, uttering every now and then a sigh, and endeavouring to look sentimental and melancholy.

All that I recollect is, that the lady, according to his account, was certainly a little touched; for she used to accept all the music that he copied for her harp, and all the patterns that he drew for her dresses; and he began to flatter himself, after a long course of delicate attentions, that he was gradually fanning up a gentle flame in her heart, when she suddenly accepted the hand of a rich, boisterous, fox-hunting baronet, without either music or sentiment, who carried her by storm, after a fortnight's courtship.

Master Simon could not help concluding by some observation upon "modest merit," and the power of gold over the sex. As a remembrance of his passion, he pointed out a heart carved on the bark of one of the trees; but which, in the process of time, had grown out into a large excrescence; and he showed me a lock of her hair, which he wore in a true lover's knot, in a large gold brooch.

I have seldom met with an old bachelor that had not, at some time or other, his nonsensical moment, when he would become tender and sentimental, talk about the concerns of the heart, and have some confession of a delicate nature to make.

Almost every man has some little trait of romance in his life, which he looks back too with fondness, and about which he is apt to grow garrulous occasionally. He recollects himself as he was at the time, young and gamesome; and forgets that his hearers have no other idea of the hero of the tale but such as he may appear at the time of telling it; peradventure, a withered, whimsical, spindle-shanked old gentleman. With married men, it is true, this is not so frequently the case; their amorous romance is apt to decline after marriage; why, I cannot for the life of me imagine; but with a bachelor, though it may slumber, it never dies. It is always liable to break out again in transient flashes, and never so much as on a spring morning in the country; or on a winter evening, when seated in his solitary chamber, stirring up the fire and talking of matrimony.

The moment that Master Simon had gone through his confession, and, to use the common phrase, "had made a clean breast of it," he became quite himself again. He had settled the point which had been worrying his mind, and doubtless considered himself established as a man of sentiment in my opinion.

Before we had finished our morning's stroll he was singing as blithe as a grasshopper, whistling to his dogs, and telling droll stories; and I recollect that he was particularly facetious that day at dinner on the subject of matrimony, and uttered several excellent jokes, not to be found in Joe Miller, that made the bride-elect blush and look down, but set all the old gentlemen at the table in a roar, and absolutely brought tears into the general's eyes.

GIPSIES

What's that to absolute freedom, such as the very beggars have; to feast and revel here to-day, and yonder to-morrow; next day where they please; and so on still, the whole country or kingdom over? There's liberty! the birds of the air can take no more.
Jovial Crew.

SINCE the meeting with the gipsies, which I have related in a former paper, I have observed several of them haunting the purlieus of the Hall, in spite of a positive interdiction of the Squire. They are part of a gang that has long kept about this neighbourhood, to the great annoyance of the farmers, whose poultry-yards often suffer from their nocturnal invasions. They are, however, in some measure patronised by the Squire, who considers the race as belonging to the good old times; which, to confess the private truth, seem to have abounded with good-for-nothing characters.

This roving crew is called "Starlight Tom's Gang," from the name of its chieftain, a notorious poacher. I have heard repeatedly of the misdeeds of this "minion of the moon;" for every midnight depredation that takes place in park, or fold, or farmyard, is laid to his charge. Starlight Tom, in fact, answers to his name; he seems to walk in darkness, and, like a fox, to be traced in the morning by the mischief he has done. He reminds me of that fearful personage in the nursery rhyme:

> "Who goes round the house at night?
> None but bloody Tom!
> Who steals all the sheep at night?
> None but one by one!"

In short, Starlight Tom is the scapegoat of the neighbourhood; but so cunning and adroit, that there is no detecting him. Old Christy and the gamekeeper have watched many a night in hopes of entrapping him; and Christy often patrols the park with his dogs, for the purpose, but all in vain. It is said that the Squire winks hard at his misdeeds, having an indulgent feeling towards the vagabond, because of his being very expert at all kinds of games, a great shot with the cross-bow, and the best morris dancer in the country.

The Squire also suffers the gang to lurk unmolested about the skirts of his estate, on condition that they do not come about the house. The approaching wedding, however, has made a kind of Saturnalia at the Hall, and has caused a suspension of all sober rule. It has produced a great sensation throughout the female part of the household; not a housemaid but dreams of wedding favours, and has a husband running in her head. Such a time is a harvest for the gipsies: there is a public footpath leading across one part of the park, by which they have free ingress, and they are continually hovering about the grounds, telling the servant girls' fortunes, or getting smuggled in to the young ladies.

I believe the Oxonian amuses himself very much by furnishing them with hints in private, and bewildering all the weak brains in the house with their wonderful revelations. The general certainly was very much astonished by the communications made to him the other evening by the gipsy girl:

he kept a wary silence towards us on the subject, and affected to treat it lightly; but I have noticed that he has since redoubled his attentions to Lady Lillycraft and her dogs.

I have seen also Phœbe Wilkins, the housekeeper's pretty and love-sick niece, holding a long conference with one of these old sibyls behind a large tree in the avenue, and often looking round to see that she was not observed. I make no doubt that she was endeavouring to get some favourable augury about the result of her love quarrel with young Ready-Money, as oracles have always been more consulted on love affairs than upon anything else. I fear, however, that in this instance the response was not so favourable as usual, for I perceived poor Phœbe returning pensively towards the house: her head hanging down, her hat in her hand, and the riband trailing along the ground.

At another time, as I turned a corner of a terrace, at the bottom of the garden, just by a clump of trees, and a large stone urn, I came upon a bevy of the young girls of the family, attended by this same Phœbe Wilkins. I was at a loss to comprehend the meaning of their blushing and giggling, and their apparent agitation, until I saw the red cloak of a gipsy vanishing among the shrubbery. A few moments after, I caught sight of Master Simon and the Oxonian stealing along one of the walks of the garden, chuckling and laughing at their successful waggery ; having evidently put the gipsy up to the thing, and instructed her what to say.

After all, there is something strangely pleasing in these tamperings with the future, even where we are convinced of the fallacy of the prediction. It is singular how willingly the mind will half deceive itself, and with what a degree of awe we will listen even to these babblers about futurity. For my part, I cannot feel angry with these poor vagabonds, that seek to deceive us into bright hopes and expectations. I have always been something of a castle-builder, and have found my liveliest pleasures to arise from the illusions which fancy has cast over commonplace realities. As I get on in life I find it more difficult to deceive myself in this delightful manner ; and I should be thankful to any prophet, however false, that would conjure the clouds which hang over futurity into palaces, and all its doubtful regions into fairyland.

The Squire, who, as I have observed, has a private goodwill towards gipsies, has suffered considerable annoyance on their account. Not that they requite his indulgence with ingratitude, for they do not depredate very flagrantly on his estate ; but because their pilferings and misdeeds occasion loud murmurs in the village. I can readily understand the old gentleman's humour on this point : I have a great toleration for all kinds of vagrant, sunshiny existence, and must confess I take a pleasure in observing the ways of gipsies. The English, who are accustomed to them from childhood, and often suffer from their petty depredations, consider them as mere nuisances : but I have been very much struck with their peculiarities. I like to behold their clear olive complexions, their romantic black eyes, their raven locks, their lithe, slender figures, and to hear them, in low silver tones, dealing forth magnificent promises of honours and estates, of world's worth, and ladies' love.

Their mode of life, too, has something in it very fanciful and picturesque. They are the free denizens of nature, and maintain a primitive independence, in spite of law and gospel; of county gaols and country magistrates. It is curious to see the obstinate adherence to the wild, unsettled habits of savage life transmitted from generation to generation, and preserved in the midst of one of the most cultivated, populous, and systematic countries in the world. They are totally distinct from the busy, thrifty people about them. They seem to be like the Indians of America, either above or below the ordinary cares and anxieties of mankind. Heedless of power, of honours, of wealth; and indifferent to the fluctuations of the times, the rise or fall of grain, or stock, or empires, they seem to laugh at the toiling, fretting world around them, and to live according to the philosophy of the old song :

> "Who would ambition shun,
> And loves to lie i' the sun,
> Seeking the food he eats,
> And pleased with what he gets.
> Come hither, come hither, come hither :
>   Here shall he see
>   No enemy,
> But winter and rough weather."

In this way they wander from county to county, keeping about the purlieus of villages, or in plenteous neighbourhoods, where there are fat farms and rich country seats. Their encampments are generally made in some beautiful spot; either a green shady nook of a road; or on the border of a common, under a sheltering hedge; or on the skirts of a fine spreading wood. They are always to be found lurking about fairs and races, and rustic gatherings, wherever there is pleasure, and throng, and idleness. They are the oracles of milkmaids and simple serving girls; and sometimes have even the honour of perusing the white hands of gentlemen's daughters, when rambling about their father's grounds. They are the bane of good housewives and thrifty farmers, and odious in the eyes of country justices; but, like all other vagabond beings, they have something to commend them to the fancy. They are among the last traces, in these matter-of-fact days, of the motley population of former times; and are whimsically associated in my mind with fairies and witches, Robin Goodfellow, Robin Hood, and the other fantastical personages of poetry.

VILLAGE WORTHIES

> Nay, I tell you, I am so well beloved in our town, that not the worst dog in the street would hurt my little finger.
>
> Collier of Croydon.

As the neighbouring village is one of those out-of-the-way, but gossiping little places, where a small matter makes a great stir, it is not to be supposed that the approach of a festival like that of May-Day can be regarded with indifference, especially since it is made a matter of such moment by the great folks at the Hall. Master Simon, who is the faithful factotum of the worthy Squire, and jumps with his humour in everything, is frequent just now in his visits to the village, to give directions for the impending fête; and as I have taken the liberty occasionally of accompanying him, I have been enabled to get some insight into the characters and internal politics of this very sagacious little community.

Master Simon is in fact the Cæsar of the village. It is true the Squire is the protecting power, but his factotum is the active and busy agent. He intermeddles in all its concerns, is acquainted with all the inhabitants and their domestic history, gives counsel to the old folks in their business matters, and the young folks in their love affairs, and enjoys the proud satisfaction of being a great man in a little world.

He is the dispenser, too, of the Squire's charity, which is bounteous; and, to do Master Simon justice, he performs this part of his functions with great alacrity. Indeed I have been entertained with the mixture of bustle, importance, and kind-heartedness which he displays. He is of too vivacious a temperament to comfort the afflicted by sitting down moping and whining and blowing noses in concert; but goes whisking about like a sparrow, chirping consolation into every hole and corner of the village. I have seen an old woman, in a red cloak, hold him for half an hour together with some long phthisical tale of distress, which Master Simon listened to with many a bob of the head, smack of his dog-whip, and other symptoms of impatience, though he afterwards made a most faithful and circumstantial report of the case to the Squire. I have watched him, too, during one of his pop visits into the cottage of a superannuated villager who is a pensioner of the Squire, when he fidgeted about the room without sitting down, made many excellent off-hand reflections with the old invalid, who was propped up in his chair, about the shortness of life, the certainty of death, and the necessity of preparing for "that awful change;" quoted several texts of Scripture very

incorrectly, but much to the edification of the cottager's wife; and on coming out pinched the daughter's rosy cheek, and wondered what was in the young men, that such a pretty face did not get a husband.

He has also his cabinet councillors in the village, with whom he is very busy just now, preparing for the May-Day ceremonies. Among these is the village tailor, a pale-faced fellow, that plays the clarionet in the church choir; and, being a great musical genius, has frequent meetings of the band at his house, where they "make night hideous" by their concerts. He is, in consequence, high in favour with Master Simon; and, through his influence, has the making, or rather marring, of all the liveries of the Hall; which generally look as though they had been cut out by one of those scientific tailors of the Flying Island of Laputa, who took measure of their customers with a quadrant. The tailor, in fact, might rise to be one of the monied men of the village, was he not rather too prone to gossip, and keep holidays, and give concerts, and blow all his substance, real and personal, through his clarionet, which literally keeps him poor both in body and estate. He has for the present thrown by all his regular work, and suffered the breeches of the village to go unmade and unmended, while he is occupied in making garlands of parti-coloured rags, in imitation of flowers, for the decoration of the May-pole.

Another of Master Simon's councillors is the apothecary, a short, and rather fat man, with a pair of prominent eyes, that diverge like those of a lobster. He is the village wise man; very sententious; and full of profound remarks on shallow subjects. Master Simon often quotes his sayings, and mentions him as rather an extraordinary man; and even consults him occasionally in desperate cases of the dogs and horses. Indeed he seems to have been overwhelmed by the apothecary's philosophy, which is exactly one observation deep, consisting of indisputable maxims, such as may be gathered from the mottoes of tobacco boxes. I had a specimen of his philosophy in my very first conversation with him; in the course of which he observed, with great solemnity and emphasis, that "man is a compound of wisdom and folly;" upon which Master Simon, who had hold of my arm, pressed very hard upon it, and whispered in my ear, "That's a devilish shrewd remark!"

THE SCHOOLMASTER

> There will no mosse stick to the stone of Sisiphus, no grasse hang on the heels of Mercury, no butter cleave on the bread of a traveller. For as the eagle at every flight loseth a feather, which maketh her bauld in her age, so the traveller in every country loseth some fleece, which maketh him a beggar in his youth, by buying that for a pound which he cannot sell again for a penny—repentance.
>
> <div align="right">LILLY's <i>Euphues</i>.</div>

AMONG the worthies of the village that enjoy the peculiar confidence of Master Simon, is one who has struck my fancy so much that I have thought him worthy of a separate notice. It is Slingsby, the schoolmaster, a thin, elderly man, rather threadbare and slovenly, somewhat indolent in manner, and with an easy, good-humoured look, not often met with in his craft. I have been interested in his favour by a few anecdotes which I have picked up concerning him.

He is a native of the village, and was a contemporary and playmate of Ready-Money Jack in the days of their boyhood. Indeed, they carried on a kind of league of mutual good offices. Slingsby was rather puny, and withal somewhat of a coward, but very apt at his learning; Jack, on the contrary, was a bully boy out of doors, but a sad laggard at his books. Slingsby helped Jack, therefore, to all his lessons: Jack fought all Slingsby's battles; and they were inseparable friends. This mutual kindness continued even after they left school, notwithstanding the dissimilarity of their characters. Jack took to ploughing and reaping, and prepared himself to till his paternal acres; while the other loitered negligently on in the path of learning, until he penetrated even into the confines of Latin and mathematics.

In an unlucky hour, however, he took to reading voyages and travels, and was smitten with a desire to see the world. This desire increased upon him as he grew up; so, early one bright, sunny morning, he put all his effects in a knapsack, slung it on his back, took staff in hand, and called in his way to take leave of his early schoolmate. Jack was just going out with the plough: the friends shook hands over the farm-house gate; Jack drove his team afield, and Slingsby whistled "Over the hills, and far away," and sallied forth gaily "to seek his fortune."

Years and years passed by, and young Tom Slingsby was forgotten: when one mellow Sunday afternoon in autumn, a thin man, somewhat advanced in life, with a coat out at elbows, a pair of old nankeen gaiters, and a few things tied in a handkerchief and slung on the end of a stick, was seen loitering through the village. He appeared to regard several houses attentively, to peer into the windows that were open, to eye the villagers wistfully as they returned from church, and then to pass some time in the churchyard reading the tombstones.

At length he found his way to the farm-house of Ready-Money Jack, but paused ere he attempted the wicket; contemplating the picture of substantial independence before him. In the porch of the house sat Ready-Money Jack, in his Sunday dress, with his hat upon his head, his pipe in his mouth, and his tankard before him, the monarch of all he surveyed. Beside him lay his fat house-dog. The varied sounds of poultry were heard from the well-stocked farm-yard; the bees hummed from their hives in the garden; the cattle lowed in the rich meadow: while the crammed barns and ample stacks bore proof of an abundant harvest.

The stranger opened the gate and advanced dubiously

towards the house. The mastiff growled at the sight of the suspicious-looking intruder, but was immediately silenced by his master, who, taking his pipe from his mouth, awaited with inquiring aspect the address of this equivocal personage. The stranger eyed old Jack for a moment, so portly in his dimensions, and decked out in gorgeous apparel; then cast a glance upon his own threadbare and starveling condition, and the scanty bundle which he held in his hand; then giving his shrunk waistcoat a twitch to make it meet his receding waistband; and casting another look, half sad, half humorous at the sturdy yeoman, "I suppose," said he, "Mr. Tibbets, you have forgot old times and old playmates?"

The latter gazed at him with scrutinising look, but acknowledged that he had no recollection of him.

"Like enough, like enough," said the stranger; "everybody seems to have forgotten poor Slingsby?"

"Why, no sure! it can't be Tom Slingsby?"

"Yes, but it is, though!" replied the stranger, shaking his head.

Ready-Money Jack was on his feet in a twinkling; thrust out his hand, gave his ancient crony the gripe of a giant, and slapping the other hand on a bench, "Sit down there," cried he, "Tom Slingsby!"

A long conversation ensued about old times, while Slingsby was regaled with the best cheer that the farm-house afforded; for he was hungry as well as wayworn, and had the keen appetite of a poor pedestrian. The early playmates then talked over their subsequent lives and adventures. Jack had but little to relate, and was never good at a long story. A prosperous life passed at home has little incident for narrative; it is only poor devils, that are tossed about the world, that are the true heroes of story. Jack had stuck by the paternal farm, followed the same plough that his forefathers had driven, and had waxed richer and richer as he grew older. As to Tom

'Why, no sure! it can't be Tom Slingsby?'

Slingsby, he was an exemplification of the old proverb, "A rolling stone gathers no moss." He had sought his fortune about the world, without ever finding it, being a thing oftener found at home than abroad. He had been in all kinds of situations, and had learned a dozen different modes of making a living; but had found his way back to his native village rather poorer than when he left it, his knapsack having dwindled down to a scanty bundle.

As luck would have it, the Squire was passing by the farm-house that very evening, and called there, as is often his custom. He found the two schoolmates still gossiping in the porch, and according to the good old Scottish song, "taking a cup of kindness yet, for auld lang syne." The Squire was struck by the contrast in appearance and fortunes of these early playmates. Ready-Money Jack, seated in lordly state, surrounded by the good things of this life, with golden guineas hanging to his very watch-chain, and the poor pilgrim Slingsby, thin as a weasel, with all his worldly effects, his bundle, hat, and walking-staff, lying on the ground beside him.

The good Squire's heart warmed towards the luckless cosmopolite, for he is a little prone to like such half-vagrant characters. He cast about in his mind how he should contrive once more to anchor Slingsby in his native village. Honest Jack had already offered him a present shelter under his roof, in spite of the hints, and winks, and half remonstrances of the shrewd Dame Tibbets; but how to provide for his permanent maintenance was the question. Luckily the Squire bethought himself that the village school was without a teacher. A little further conversation convinced him that Slingsby was as fit for that as for anything else, and in a day or two he was seen swaying the rod of empire in the very school-house where he had often been horsed in the days of his boyhood.

Here he has remained for several years, and being honoured by the countenance of the Squire, and the fast friendship of

Mr. Tibbets, he has grown into much importance and consideration in the village. I am told, however, that he still shows, now and then, a degree of restlessness, and a disposition to rove abroad again, and see a little more of the world; an inclination which seems particularly to haunt him about spring-time. There is nothing so difficult to conquer as the vagrant humour, when once it has been fully indulged.

Since I have heard these anecdotes of poor Slingsby, I have more than once mused upon the picture presented by him and his schoolmate Ready-Money Jack, on their coming together again after so long a separation. It is difficult to determine between lots in life, where each is attended with its peculiar discontents. He who never leaves his home repines at his monotonous existence, and envies the traveller, whose life is a constant tissue of wonder and adventure; while he,

who is tossed about the world, looks back with many a sigh to the safe and quiet shore which he has abandoned. I cannot help thinking, however, that the man that stays at home, and cultivates the comforts and pleasures daily springing up around him, stands the best chance for happiness. There is nothing so fascinating to a young mind as the idea of travelling; and there is very witchcraft in the old phrase found in every nursery tale, of "going to seek one's fortune." A continual change of place, and change of object, promises a continual succession of adventure and gratification of curiosity. But there is a limit to all our enjoyments, and every desire bears its death in its very gratification. Curiosity languishes under repeated stimulants, novelties cease to excite surprise, until at length we cannot wonder even at a miracle. He who has sallied forth into the world, like poor Slingsby, full of sunny anticipations, finds too soon how different the distant scene becomes when visited. The smooth place roughens as he approaches; the wild place becomes tame and barren; the fairy tints that beguiled him on still fly to the distant hill, or gather upon the land he has left behind, and every part of the landscape seems greener than the spot he stands on.

THE SCHOOL.

But to come down from great men and higher matters to my little children and poor school-house again; I will, God willing, go forward orderly, as I proposed, to instruct children and young men both for learning and manners.

ROGER ASCHAM.

HAVING given the reader a slight sketch of the village schoolmaster, he may be curious to learn something concerning his school. As the Squire takes much interest in the education of the neighbouring children, he put into the hands of the teacher, on first installing him in office, a copy of Roger Ascham's School-master, and advised him, moreover, to con over that portion of old Peachum which treats of the duty of masters, and which condemns the favourite method of making boys wise by flagellation.

He exhorted Slingsby not to break down or depress the free spirit of the boys by harshness and slavish fear, but to lead them freely and joyously on in the path of knowledge, making it pleasant and desirable in their eyes. He wished to see the youth trained up in the manners and habitudes of the peasantry of the good old times, and thus to lay the foundation for the accomplishment of his favourite object, the revival of old English customs and character. He recommended that all the ancient holidays should be observed, and that the sports of the boys, in their hours of play, should be regulated according to the standard authorities laid down by Strutt; a copy of whose invaluable work, decorated with plates, was deposited in the school-house. Above all, he exhorted the pedagogue to abstain from the use of birch, an instrument of instruction which the good Squire regards with abhorrence, as fit only for the coercion of brute natures, that cannot be reasoned with.

Mr. Slingsby has followed the Squire's instructions to the best of his disposition and abilities. He never flogs the boys, because he is too easy, good-humoured a creature to inflict pain on a worm. He is bountiful in holidays, because he loves holidays himself, and has a sympathy with the urchins' impatience of confinement, from having divers times experienced its irksomeness during the time that he was seeing the world. As to sports and pastimes, the boys are faithfully exercised in all that are on record,—quoits, races, prison-bars, tip-cat, trap-ball, bandy-ball, wrestling, leaping, and what not. The only misfortune is, that having banished the birch, honest Slingsby has not studied Roger Ascham sufficiently to find out a substitute, or rather he has not the management in his nature to apply one; his school, therefore, though one of the happiest, is one of the most unruly in the country; and never was a pedagogue more liked, or less heeded, by his disciples than Slingsby.

He has lately taken a coadjutor worthy of himself, being another stray sheep that has returned to the village fold. This is no other than the son of the musical tailor, who had bestowed some cost upon his education, hoping to see him one day arrive at the dignity of an exciseman, or at least of a parish clerk. The lad grew up, however, as idle and musical as his father; and being captivated by the drum and fife of a recruiting party, he followed them off to the army. He returned not long since, out of money, and out at elbows, the prodigal son of the village. He remained for some time lounging about the place in half-tattered soldier's dress, with a foraging cap on one side of his head, jerking stones across the

brook, or loitering about the tavern door, a burthen to his father, and regarded with great coldness by all warm householders.

Something, however, drew honest Slingsby towards the youth. It might be the kindness he bore to his father, who is one of the schoolmaster's greatest cronies; it might be that secret sympathy, which draws men of vagrant propensities towards each other; for there is something truly magnetic in the vagabond feeling; or it might be, that he remembered the time when he himself had come back, like this youngster, a wreck to his native place. At any rate, whatever the motive,

Slingsby drew towards the youth. They had many conversations in the village tap-room about foreign parts, and the various scenes and places they had witnessed during their wayfaring about the world. The more Slingsby talked with him, the more he found him to his taste, and finding him almost as learned as himself, he forthwith engaged him as an assistant or usher in the school.

Under such admirable tuition, the school, as may be supposed, flourishes apace; and if the scholars do not become

versed in all the holiday accomplishments of the good old times, to the Squire's heart's content, it will not be the fault of their teachers. The prodigal son has become almost as popular among the boys as the pedagogue himself. His instructions are not limited to school hours; and having inherited the musical taste and talents of his father, he has bitten the whole school with the mania. He is a great hand at beating a drum, which is often heard rumbling from the rear of the school-house. He is teaching half the boys of the village, also, to play the fife, and the pandean pipes; and they weary the whole neighbourhood with their vague piping, as they sit perched on stiles or loitering about the barn-doors in the evenings. Among the other exercises of the school, also, he has introduced the ancient art of archery, one of the Squire's favourite themes, with such success, that the whipsters roam in truant bands about the neighbourhood, practising with their bows and arrows upon the birds of the air, and the beasts of the field; and not unfrequently making a foray into the Squire's domains, to the great indignation of the gamekeepers. In a word, so completely are the ancient English customs and habits cultivated at this school, that I should not be surprised if the Squire should live to see one of his poetic visions realised, and a brood reared up, worthy successors to Robin Hood and his merry gang of outlaws.

A VILLAGE POLITICIAN

I am a rogue if I do not think I was designed for the helm of state; I am so full of nimble stratagems, that I should have ordered affairs, and carried it against the stream of a faction, with as much ease as a skipper would laver against the wind.
The Goblins.

IN one of my visits to the village with Master Simon, he proposed that we should stop at the inn, which he wished to show me, as a specimen of a real country inn, the head-quarters of village gossip. I had remarked it before, in my perambulations about the place. It has a deep, old-fashioned porch, leading into a large hall, which serves for tap-room and travellers' room; having a wide fireplace, with high-backed settles on each side, where the wise men of the village gossip over their ale, and hold their sessions during the long winter evenings. The landlord is an easy, indolent fellow, shaped a little like one of his own beer barrels, and is apt to stand gossiping at his door, with his wig on one side, and his hands in his pockets, whilst his wife and daughter attend to customers. His wife, however, is fully competent to manage the establishment; and, indeed, from long habitude, rules over all the frequenters of the tap-room as completely as if they were her dependants instead of her patrons. Not a veteran ale-bibber but pays homage to her, having, no doubt, been often in her arrears. I have already hinted that she is on very good terms with Ready-Money Jack. He was a sweetheart of hers in early life, and has always countenanced the tavern on her account. Indeed, he is quite "the cock of the walk" at the tap-room.

As we approached the inn, we heard some one talking with great volubility, and distinguished the ominous words "taxes," "poor's rates," and "agricultural distress." It proved to be a thin, loquacious fellow, who had penned the landlord up in one corner of the porch, with his hands in his pockets, as usual, listening with an air of the most vacant acquiescence.

The sight seemed to have a curious effect on Master Simon, as he squeezed my arm, and, altering his course, sheered wide of the porch as though he had not had any idea of entering. This evident evasion induced me to notice the orator more particularly. He was meagre, but active in his make, with a long, pale, bilious face, a black, ill-shaven beard, a feverish eye, and a hat sharpened up at the sides into a most pragmatical shape. He had a newspaper in his hand, and seemed to be commenting on its contents, to the thorough conviction of mine host.

At sight of Master Simon the landlord was evidently a little flurried, and began to rub his hands, edge away from his corner, and make several profound publican bows; while the orator took no other notice of my companion than to talk rather louder than before, and with, as I thought, something of an air of defiance. Master Simon, however, as I have before said, sheered off from the porch, and passed on, pressing my arm within his, and whispering as we got by, in a tone of awe and horror, "That's a radical! he reads Cobbett!"

I endeavoured to get a more particular account of him from my companion, but he seemed unwilling even to talk about him, answering only in general terms, that he was "a cursed busy fellow, that had a confounded trick of talking, and was apt to bother one about the national debt, and such nonsense;" from which I suspected that Master Simon had been rendered wary of him by some accidental encounter on the field of argument: for these radicals are continually roving about in quest of wordy warfare, and never so happy as when they can tilt a gentleman logician out of his saddle.

On subsequent inquiry my suspicions have been confirmed. I find the radical has but recently found his way into the village, where he threatens to commit fearful devastations with his doctrines. He has already made two or three complete converts, or new lights: has shaken the faith of several others; and has grievously puzzled the brains of many of the oldest villagers, who had never thought about politics, or scarce anything else, during their whole lives.

He is lean and meagre from the constant restlessness of mind and body; worrying about with newspapers and pamphlets in his pockets, which he is ready to pull out on all occasions. He has shocked several of the staunchest villagers by talking lightly of the Squire and his family; and hinting that it would be better the park should be cut up into small farms and kitchen gardens, or feed good mutton instead of worthless deer.

He is a great thorn in the side of the Squire, who is sadly afraid that he will introduce politics into the village, and turn it into an unhappy, thinking community. He is a still greater grievance to Master Simon, who has hitherto been able to sway

the political opinions of the place, without much cost of learning or logic; but has been very much puzzled of late to weed out the doubts and heresies already sown by this champion of reform. Indeed, the latter has taken complete command at the tap-room of the tavern, not so much because he has convinced, as because he has out-talked all the established oracles. The apothecary, with all his philosophy, was as nought before him. He has convinced and converted the landlord at least a dozen times; who, however, is liable to be convinced and converted the other way by the next person with whom he talks. It is true the radical has a violent antagonist in the landlady, who is vehemently loyal, and thoroughly devoted to the king, Master Simon, and the Squire. She now and then comes out upon the reformer with all the fierceness of a cat-o'-mountain, and does not spare her own soft-headed husband, for listening to what she terms such "low-lived politics." What makes the good woman the more violent, is the perfect coolness with which the radical listens to her attacks, drawing his face up into a provoking supercilious smile; and when she has talked herself out of breath, quietly asking her for a taste of her home-brewed.

The only person who is in any way a match for this redoubtable politician is Ready-Money Jack Tibbets, who maintains his stand in the tap-room, in defiance of the radical and all his works. Jack is one of the most loyal men in the country, without being able to reason about the matter. He has that admirable quality for a tough arguer, also, that he never knows when he is beat. He has half a dozen old maxims, which he advances on all occasions, and though his antagonist may overturn them never so often, yet he always brings them anew into the field. He is like the robber in Ariosto, who, though his head might be cut off half a hundred times, yet whipt it on his shoulders again in a twinkling, and returned as sound a man as ever to the charge.

Whatever does not square with Jack's simple and obvious creed, he sets down for "French politics;" for, notwithstanding the peace, he cannot be persuaded that the French are not still laying plots to ruin the nation, and to get hold of the Bank of England. The radical attempted to overwhelm him one day by a long passage from a newspaper; but Jack neither reads nor believes on newspapers. In reply he gave him one of the stanzas which he has by heart from his favourite, and indeed only author, old Tusser, and which he calls his Golden Rules:

> Leave Princes' affairs undescanted on,
> And tend to such doings as stand thee upon;
> Fear God, and offend not the King nor his laws,
> And keep thyself out of the magistrate's claws.

When Tibbets had pronounced this with great emphasis, he pulled out a well-filled leathern purse, took out a handful of gold and silver, paid his score at the bar with great punctuality, returned his money, piece by piece, into his purse, his purse into his pocket, which he buttoned up, and then giving his cudgel a stout thump upon the floor, and bidding the radical "Good morning, sir!" with the tone of a man who conceives he has completely done for his antagonist, he walked with lion-like gravity out of the house. Two or three of Jack's admirers who were present, and had been afraid to take the field themselves, looked upon this as a perfect triumph, and winked at each other when the radical's back was turned. "Ay, ay!" said mine host, as soon as the radical was out of hearing, "let old Jack alone; I'll warrant he'll give him his own!"

THE ROOKERY

But cawing rooks, and kites that swim sublime
In still repeated circles, screaming loud,
The jay, the pie, and e'en the boding owl,
That hails the rising moon, have charms for me.
                                                    COWPER.

IN a grove of tall oaks and beeches, that crowns a terrace walk, just on the skirts of the garden, is an ancient rookery, which is one of the most important provinces in the Squire's rural domains. The old gentleman sets great store by his rooks, and will not suffer one of them to be killed, in consequence of which they have increased amazingly; the tree tops are loaded with their nests; they have encroached upon the great avenue, and have even established, in times long past, a colony among the elms and pines of the churchyard, which, like other distant colonies, has already thrown off allegiance to the mother-country.

The rooks are looked upon by the Squire as a very ancient and honourable line of gentry, highly aristocratical in their notions, fond of place, and attached to church and state; as their building so loftily, keeping about churches and cathedrals, and in the venerable groves of old castles and manor-houses, sufficiently manifests. The good opinion thus expressed by the Squire put me upon observing more narrowly these very respectable birds; for I confess, to my shame, I had been apt to confound them with their cousins-german the crows, to whom, at the first glance, they bear so great a family resemblance. Nothing, it seems, could be more unjust or injurious than such a mistake. The rooks and crows are, among the feathered tribes, what the Spaniards and the Portuguese are among nations, the least loving, in consequence of their neighbourhood and similarity. The rooks are old-established housekeepers, high-minded gentlefolk that have had their hereditary abodes time out of mind; but as to the poor crows, they are a kind of vagabond, predatory, gipsy race, roving about the country, without any settled home; "their hands are against everybody, and everybody's against them," and they are gibbeted in every corn-field. Master Simon assures me that a female rook that should so far forget herself as to consort with a crow, would inevitably be disinherited, and indeed would be totally discarded by all her genteel acquaintance.

The Squire is very watchful over the interests and concerns of his sable neighbours. As to Master Simon, he even pretends to know many of them by sight, and to have given names to them; he points out several which he says are old heads of families, and compares them to worthy old citizens, beforehand in the world, that wear cocked hats and silver buckles in their shoes. Notwithstanding the protecting benevolence of the Squire, and their being residents in his empire, they seem to acknowledge no allegiance, and to hold no intercourse or intimacy. Their airy tenements are built almost out of the reach of gunshot; and, notwithstanding their vicinity to the Hall, they maintain a most reserved and distrustful shyness of mankind.

There is one season of the year, however, which brings all birds in a manner to a level, and tames the pride of the loftiest highflyer: which is the season of building their nests. This takes place early in the spring, when the forest trees first begin to show their buds: the long withy ends of the branches to turn green; when the wild strawberry, and other herbage of the sheltered woodlands, put forth their tender and tinted leaves, and the daisy and the primrose peep from under the hedges. At this time there is a general bustle among the feathered tribes; an incessant fluttering about, and a cheerful chirping, indicative, like the germination of the vegetable world, of the reviving life and fecundity of the year.

It is then that the rooks forget their usual stateliness, and their shy and lofty habits. Instead of keeping up in the

high regions of the air, swinging on the breezy-tree tops, and looking down with sovereign contempt upon the humble crawlers upon earth, they are fain to throw off for a time the dignity of a gentleman, and to come down to the ground, and put on the painstaking and industrious character of a labourer. They now lose their natural shyness, become fearless and familiar, and may be seen flying about in all directions, with an air of great assiduity, in search of building materials. Every now and then your path will be crossed by one of these busy old gentlemen, worrying about with awkward gait, as if troubled with the gout or with corns on his toes, casting about many a prying look, turning down first one eye, then the other, in earnest consideration upon every straw he meets with, until espying some mighty twig, large enough to make a rafter for his air-castle, he will seize upon it with avidity, and hurry away with it to the tree-top; fearing, apparently, lest you should dispute with him the invaluable prize.

Like other castle-builders, these airy architects seem rather fanciful in the materials with which they build, and to like those most which come from a distance. Thus, though there are abundance of dry twigs on the surrounding trees, yet they never think of making use of them, but go foraging in distant lands, and come sailing home, one by one, from the ends of the earth, each bearing in his bill some precious piece of timber.

Nor must I avoid mentioning what, I grieve to say, rather derogates from the grave and honourable character of these ancient gentlefolk, that, during the architectural season they are subject to great dissensions among themselves : that they make no scruple to defraud and plunder each other ; and that sometimes the rookery is a scene of hideous brawl and commotion, in consequence of some delinquency of the kind. One of the partners generally remains on the nest to guard it from depredation ; and I have seen severe contests when some sly neighbour has endeavoured to filch away a tempting rafter that has captivated his eye. As I am not willing to admit any suspicion hastily that should throw a stigma on the general character of so worshipful a people, I am inclined to think that these larcenies are very much discountenanced by the higher classes, and even rigorously punished by those in authority ; for I have now and then seen a whole gang of rooks fall upon the nest of some individual, pull it all to pieces, carry off the spoils, and even buffet the luckless proprietor. I have concluded this to be some signal punishment inflicted upon him by the officers of the police, for some pilfering misdemeanour; or, perhaps, that it was a crew of bailiffs carrying an execution into his house. I have been amused with another of their movements during the building season. The steward has suffered a considerable number of sheep to graze on a lawn near the

house, somewhat to the annoyance of the Squire, who thinks this an innovation on the dignity of a park, which ought to be devoted to deer only. Be this as it may, there is a green knoll, not far from the drawing-room window, where the ewes and lambs are accustomed to assemble towards evening for the benefit of the setting sun. No sooner were they gathered here, at the time when these politic birds were building, than a stately old rook, who, Master Simon assured me, was the chief magistrate of this community, would settle down upon the head of one of the ewes, who, seeming conscious of this condescension, would desist from grazing, and stand fixed in motionless reverence of her august brethren: the rest of the rookery would then come wheeling down, in imitation of their leader, until every ewe had two or three of them cawing, and fluttering, and battling upon her back. Whether they requited the submission of the sheep by levying a contribution upon their fleece for the benefit of the rookery, I am not certain, though I presume they followed the usual custom of protecting powers.

The latter part of May is a time of great tribulation among the rookeries, when the young are just able to leave the nests, and balance themselves on the neighbouring branches. Now comes on the season of "rook shooting;" a terrible slaughter of the innocents. The Squire, of course, prohibits all invasion of the kind on his territories; but I am told that a lamentable havoc takes place in the colony about the old church. Upon this devoted commonwealth the village charges "with all its chivalry." Every idle wight that is lucky enough to possess an old gun or a blunderbuss, together with all the archery of Slingsby's school, take the field on the occasion. In vain does the little parson interfere, or remonstrate in angry tones, from his study window that looks into the churchyard; there is a continual popping from morning to night. Being no great marksmen, their shots are not often effective; but every now and then a great shout from the besieging army of bumpkins makes known the downfall of some unlucky, squab rook, which comes to the ground with the emphasis of a squashed apple-dumpling.

Nor is the rookery entirely free from other troubles and disasters. In so aristocratical and lofty-minded a community, which boasts so much ancient blood and hereditary pride, it is natural to suppose that questions of etiquette will sometimes arise, and affairs of honour ensue. In fact, this is very often the case: bitter quarrels break out between individuals, which produce sad scufflings on the tree-tops, and I have more than once seen a regular duel take place between two doughty heroes of the rookery. Their field of battle is generally the air; and their contest is managed in the most scientific and elegant manner; wheeling round and round each other, and towering higher and higher to get the vantage ground, until they sometimes disappear in the clouds before the combat is determined. They have also fierce combats now and then with an invading hawk, and will drive him off from their territories by a *posse comitatus*. They are also extremely tenacious of their domains, and will suffer no other bird to inhabit the grove or its vicinity. There was a very ancient and respectable old bachelor owl that had long had his lodgings in a corner of the grove, but has been fairly ejected by the rooks, and has retired, disgusted with the world, to a neighbouring wood, where he leads the life of a hermit, and makes nightly complaints of his ill-treatment.

The hootings of this unhappy gentleman may generally be heard in the still evenings, when the rooks are all at rest: and I have often listened to them of a moonlight night, with a kind of mysterious gratification. This gray-bearded misanthrope of course is highly respected by the Squire, but the servants have superstitious notions about him; and it would be difficult to get the dairymaid to venture after dark near to the wood which he inhabits.

Besides the private quarrels of the rooks, there are other misfortunes to which they are liable, and which often bring distress into the most respectable families of the rookery. Having the true baronial spirit of the good old feudal times, they are apt now and then to issue forth from their castles on a foray, and to lay the plebeian fields of the neighbouring country under contribution; in the course of which chivalrous expeditions they now and then get a shot from the rusty artillery of some refractory farmer. Occasionally, too, while they are quietly taking the air beyond the park boundaries, they have the incaution to come within the reach of the truant bowmen of Slingsby's school, and receive a flight shot from some unlucky urchin's arrow. In such case the wounded adventurer will sometimes have just strength enough to bring himself home, and, giving up the ghost at the rookery, will hang dangling "all abroad" on a bough like a thief on a gibbet; an awful warning to his friends, and an object of great commiseration to the Squire. But, maugre all these untoward incidents, the rooks have, upon the whole, a happy holiday life of it. When their young are reared, and fairly launched upon their native element, the air, the cares of the old folks seem over, and they resume all their aristocratical dignity and idleness. I have envied them the enjoyment which they appear to have in their ethereal heights, sporting with clamorous exultation about their lofty bowers; sometimes hovering over them, sometimes partially alighting upon the topmost branches, and there balancing with outstretched wings, and swinging in the breeze. Sometimes they seem to take a fashionable drive to the church, and amuse themselves by circling in airy rings about its spire: at other times a mere garrison is left at home to mount guard in their stronghold at the grove, while the rest roam abroad to enjoy the fine weather. About sunset the garrison gives notice of their return; their faint cawing will be heard from a great distance, and they will be seen far off like a sable cloud, and then nearer and nearer, until they all come soaring home. Then they perform several grand circuits in the air, over the Hall and garden, wheeling closer and closer, until they gradually settle down upon the grove, when a prodigious cawing takes place, as though they were relating their day's adventures.

I like at such times to walk about these dusky groves, and hear the various sounds of these airy people roosted so high above me. As the gloom increases, their conversation subsides, and they seem to be gradually dropping asleep; but every now and then there is a querulous note, as if some one was quarrelling for a pillow, or a little more of the blanket. It is late in the evening before they completely sink to repose, and then their old anchorite neighbour, the owl, begins his lonely hootings from his bachelor's hall in the wood.

MAY-DAY

It is the choice time of the year,
For the violets now appear;
Now the rose receives its birth,
And pretty primrose decks the earth,
 Then to the May-pole come away,
 For it is now a holiday.

Actæon and Diana.

As I was lying in bed this morning, enjoying one of those half-dreams, half-reveries, which are so pleasant in the country, when the birds are singing about the window, and the sunbeams peeping through the curtains, I was roused by the sound of music. On going down-stairs, I found a number of villagers dressed in their holiday clothes, bearing a pole ornamented with garlands and ribands, and accompanied by the village band of music, under the direction of the tailor, the pale fellow who plays on the clarionet. They had all sprigs of hawthorn, or, as it is called, "the May," in their hats, and had brought green branches and flowers to decorate the Hall door and windows. They had come to give notice that the May-pole was reared on the green, and to invite the household to witness the sports. The Hall, according to custom, became a scene of hurry and delightful confusion. The servants were all agog with May and music; and there was no keeping either the tongues or the feet of the maids quiet, who were anticipating the sports of the green, and the evening dance.

I repaired to the village at an early hour to enjoy the merry-making. The morning was pure and sunny, such as a May morning is always described. The fields were white with daisies, the hawthorn was covered with its fragrant blossoms, the bee hummed about every bank, and the swallow played high in the air about the village steeple. It was one of those genial days when we seem to draw in pleasure with the very air we breathe, and to feel happy we know not why. Whoever has felt the worth of worthy man, or has doted on lovely woman, will, on such a day, call them tenderly to mind, and feel his heart all alive with long-buried recollections. "For thenne," says the excellent romance of King Arthur, "lovers call ageyne to their mynde old gentilnes and old servyse, and many kind dedes that were forgotten by neglygence."

Before reaching the village, I saw the May-pole towering above the cottages, with its gay garlands and streamers, and heard the sound of music. I found that there had been booths set up near it, for the reception of company; and a bower of green branches and flowers for the Queen of May, a fresh, rosy-cheeked girl of the village.

A band of morris-dancers were capering on the green in their fantastic dresses, jingling with hawks' bells, with a boy dressed up as Maid Marian, and the attendant fool rattling his box to collect contributions from the bystanders. The gipsy women, too, were already plying their mystery in by-corners of the village, reading the hands of the simple country girls, and no doubt promising them all good husbands and tribes of children.

The Squire made his appearance in the course of the morning, attended by the parson, and was received with loud acclamations. He mingled among the country people throughout the day, giving and receiving pleasure wherever he went. The amusements of the day were under the management of Slingsby, the schoolmaster, who is not merely lord of misrule in his school, but master of the revels to the village. He was bustling about with the perplexed and anxious air of a man who has the oppressive burthen of promoting other people's

merriment upon his mind. He had involved himself in a dozen scrapes in consequence of a politic intrigue, which, by the by, Master Simon and the Oxonian were at the bottom of, which had for object the election of the Queen of May. He had met with violent opposition from a faction of ale-drinkers, who were in favour of a bouncing barmaid, the daughter of the innkeeper; but he had been too strongly backed not to carry his point, though it shows that these rural crowns, like all others, are objects of great ambition and heart-burning. I am told that Master Simon takes great interest, though in an underhand way, in the election of these May-Day Queens, and that the chaplet is generally secured for some rustic beauty that has found favour in his eyes. In the course of the day there were various games of strength and agility on the green, at which a knot of village veterans presided, as judges of the lists. Among those I perceived that Ready-Money Jack took the lead, looking with a learned and critical eye on the merits of the different candidates; and though he was very laconic, and sometimes merely expressed himself by a nod, yet it was evident that his opinions far outweighed those of the most loquacious.

Young Jack Tibbets was the hero of the day, and carried off most of the prizes, though in some of the feats of agility he was rivalled by the "prodigal son," who appeared much in his element on this occasion; but his most formidable competitor was the notorious gipsy, the redoubtable "Starlight Tom." I was rejoiced at having an opportunity of seeing this "minion of the moon" in broad daylight. I found him a tall, swarthy, good-looking fellow, with a lofty air, something like what I have seen in an Indian chieftain; and with a certain lounging, easy, and almost graceful carriage, which I have often remarked in beings of the lazzaroni order, that lead an idle loitering life, and have a gentleman-like contempt of labour.

Master Simon and the old general reconnoitred the ground together, and indulged a vast deal of harmless raking among the buxom country girls. Master Simon would give some of them a kiss on meeting with them, and would ask after their sisters, for he is acquainted with most of the farmers' families. Sometimes he would whisper, and affect to talk mischievously with them, and, if bantered on the subject, would turn it off with a laugh, though it was evident he liked to be suspected of being a gay Lothario amongst them.

He had much to say to the farmers about their farms, and

seemed to know all their horses by name. There was an old fellow, with a round, ruddy face, and a night-cap under his hat, the village wit, who took several occasions to crack a joke with him in the hearing of his companions, to whom he would turn and wink hard when Master Simon had passed.

The harmony of the day, however, had nearly at one time been interrupted by the appearance of the radical on the ground, with two or three of his disciples. He soon got engaged in argument in the very thick of the throng, above which I could hear his voice, and now and then see his meagre hand, half a mile out of the sleeve, elevated in the air in violent gesticulation, and flourishing a pamphlet by way of truncheon. He was decrying these idle nonsensical amusements in times of public distress, when it was every one's business to think of other matters, and to be miserable. The honest village logicians could make no stand against him, especially as he was seconded by his proselytes; when, to their great joy, Master Simon and the general came drifting down into the field of action. I saw that Master Simon was for making off, as soon as he found himself in the neighbourhood of this fireship; but the general was too loyal to suffer such talk in his hearing, and thought, no doubt, that a look and a word from a gentleman would be sufficient to shut up so shabby an orator. The latter, however, was no respecter of persons, but rather seemed to exult in having such important antagonists. He talked with greater volubility than ever, and soon drowned them with declamation on the subject of taxes, poor's rates, and the national debt. Master Simon endeavoured to brush along in his usual excursive manner, which had always answered amazingly well with the villagers; but the radical was one of those pestilent fellows that pin a man down to facts, and, indeed, he had two or three pamphlets in his pocket, to support everything he advanced by printed documents. The general, too, found himself betrayed into a more serious action than his dignity could brook, and looked like a mighty Dutch Indiaman grievously peppered by a petty privateer. It was in vain that he swelled and looked big, and talked large, and endeavoured to make up by pomp of manner for poverty of matter; every home-thrust of the radical made him wheeze like a bellows, and seemed to let a volume of wind out of him. In a word, the

two worthies from the Hall were completely dumbfounded, and this, too, in the presence of several of Master Simon's staunch admirers, who had always looked up to him as infallible. I do not know how he and the general would have managed to draw their forces decently from the field, had there not been a match at grinning through a horse-collar announced, whereupon the radical retired with great expression of contempt, and as soon as his back was turned, the argument was carried against him all hollow.

"Did you ever hear such a pack of stuff, general?" said

Master Simon; "there's no talking with one of these chaps when he once gets that confounded Cobbett in his head."

"S'blood, sir!" said the general, wiping his forehead, "such fellows ought all to be transported!"

In the latter part of the day the ladies from the Hall paid a visit to the green. The fair Julia made her appearance, leaning on her lover's arm, and looking extremely pale and

interesting. As she is a great favourite in the village, where she has been known from childhood, and as her late accident had been much talked about, the sight of her caused very manifest delight, and some of the old women of the village blessed her sweet face as she passed.

While they were walking about, I noticed the schoolmaster in earnest conversation with the young girl that represented the Queen of May, evidently endeavouring to spirit her up to some formidable undertaking. At length, as the party from the Hall approached her bower, she came forth, faltering at every step, until she reached the spot where the fair Julia stood between her lover and Lady Lillycraft. The little Queen then took the chaplet of flowers from her head, and attempted to put it on that of the bride elect; but the confusion of both was so great, that the wreath would have fallen to the ground, had not the officer caught it, and, laughing, placed it upon the blushing brows of his mistress. There was something charming in the very embarrassment of these two young creatures, both so beautiful, yet so different in their kinds of beauty. Master Simon told me, afterwards, that the Queen of May was to have spoken a few verses which the schoolmaster had written for her; but that she had neither wit to understand nor memory to recollect them. "Besides," added he, "between you and I, she murders the king's English abominably; so she has acted the part of a wise woman in holding her tongue, and trusting to her pretty face."

Among the other characters from the Hall was Mrs. Hannah, my Lady Lillycraft's gentlewoman: to my surprise she was escorted by old Christy the huntsman, and followed by his ghost of a grayhound; but I find they are very old acquaintances, being drawn together from some sympathy of disposition. Mrs. Hannah moved about with starched dignity among the rustics, who drew back from her with more awe than they did from her mistress. Her mouth seemed shut as with a clasp; excepting that I now and then heard the word "fellows" escape from between her lips, as she got accidentally jostled in the crowd.

But there was one other heart present that did not enter into the merriment of the scene, which was that of the simple Phœbe Wilkins, the housekeeper's niece. The poor girl has continued to pine and whine for some time past, in consequence of the obstinate coldness of her lover; never was a little flirtation more severely punished. She appeared this day on the green, gallanted by a smart servant out of livery, and had evidently resolved to try the hazardous experiment of awakening the jealousy of her lover. She was dressed in her very best; affected an air of great gaiety: talked loud and girlishly, and laughed when there was nothing to laugh at. There was, however, an aching, heavy heart, in the poor baggage's bosom, in spite of all her levity. Her eye turned every now and then in quest of her reckless lover, and her cheek grew pale, and her fictitious gaiety vanished, on seeing him paying his rustic homage to the little May-day Queen.

My attention was now diverted by a fresh stir and bustle. Music was heard from a distance; a banner was seen advancing up the road, preceded by a rustic band playing something like a march, and followed by a sturdy throng of country lads, the chivalry of a neighbouring and rival village.

No sooner had they reached the green than they challenged the heroes of the day to new trials of strength and activity. Several gymnastic contests ensued for the honour of the respective villages. In the course of these exercises, young Tibbets and the champion of the adverse party had an obstinate match at wrestling. They tugged, and strained, and panted, without either getting the mastery, until both came to the ground, and rolled upon the green. Just then the disconsolate Phœbe came by. She saw her recreant lover in fierce contest, as she thought, and in danger. In a moment pride, pique, and coquetry were forgotten; she rushed into the ring, seized upon the rival champion by the hair, and was on the point of wreaking on him her puny vengeance, when a buxom, strapping, country lass, the sweetheart of the prostrate swain, pounced upon her like a hawk, and would have stripped her of her fine plumage in a twinkling, had she also not been seized in her turn.

A complete tumult ensued. The chivalry of the two villages became embroiled. Blows began to be dealt, and

'A complete tumult ensued.'

sticks to be flourished. Phœbe was carried off from the field in hysterics. In vain did the sages of the village interfere. The sententious apothecary endeavoured to pour the soothing oil of his philosophy upon this tempestuous sea of passion, but was tumbled into the dust. Slingsby, the pedagogue, who is a great lover of peace, went into the middle of the throng, as marshal of the day, to put an end to the commotion, but was rent in twain, and came out with his garment hanging in two strips from his shoulders; upon which the prodigal son dashed in with fury to revenge the insult which his patron had sustained. The tumult thickened; I caught glimpses of the jockey-cap of old Christy, like the helmet of a chieftain, bobbing about in the midst of the scuffle; while Mrs. Hannah, separated from her doughty protector, was squalling and striking at right and left with a faded parasol; being tossed and tousled about by the crowd in such wise as never happened to maiden gentlewoman before.

At length I beheld old Ready-Money Jack making his way into the very thickest of the throng; tearing it, as it were, apart, and enforcing peace *vi et armis*. It was surprising to see the sudden quiet that ensued. The storm settled down at once into tranquillity. The parties, having no real grounds of hostility, were readily pacified, and in fact were a little at a loss to know why and how they had got by the ears. Slingsby was speedily stitched together again by his friend the tailor, and resumed his usual good-humour. Mrs. Hannah drew on one side to plume her rumpled feathers; and old Christy, having repaired his damages, took her under his arm, and they swept back again to the Hall, ten times more bitter against mankind than ever.

The Tibbets family alone seemed slow in recovering from the agitation of the scene. Young Jack was evidently very much moved by the heroism of the unlucky Phœbe. His mother, who had been summoned to the field of action by

news of the affray, was in a sad panic, and had need of all her management to keep him from following his mistress, and coming to a perfect reconciliation.

What heightened the alarm and perplexity of the good managing dame was, that the matter had roused the slow apprehension of old Ready-Money himself; who was very much struck by the intrepid interference of so pretty and delicate a girl, and was sadly puzzled to understand the meaning of the violent agitation in his family.

When all this came to the ears of the Squire, he was grievously scandalised that his May-day fête should have been disgraced by such a brawl. He ordered Phœbe to appear before him; but the girl was so frightened and distressed, that she came sobbing and trembling, and, at the first question he asked, fell again into hysterics. Lady Lillycraft, who had understood that there was an affair of the heart at the bottom of this distress, immediately took the girl into great favour and protection, and made her peace with the Squire. This was the only thing that disturbed the harmony of the day, if we except the discomfiture of Master Simon and the general by the radical. Upon the whole, therefore, the Squire had very fair reason to be satisfied that he had rode his hobby throughout the day without any other molestation.

The reader, learned in these matters, will perceive that all this was but a faint shadow of the once gay and fanciful rites of May. The peasantry have lost the proper feeling for these rites, and have grown almost as strange to them as the boors of La Mancha were to the customs of chivalry in the days of the valorous Don Quixote. Indeed, I considered it a proof of the discretion with which the Squire rides his hobby, that he had not pushed the thing any farther, nor attempted to revive many obsolete usages of the day, which, in the present matter-of-fact times, would appear affected and absurd. I must say, though I do it under the rose, the general brawl in which this festival had nearly terminated has made me doubt whether these rural customs of the good old times were always so very loving and innocent as we are apt to fancy them; and whether the peasantry in those times were really so Arcadian as they have been fondly represented. I begin to fear

> "Those days were never; airy dreams
> Sat for the picture, and the poet's hand,
> Imparting substance to an empty shade
> Imposed a gay delirium for a truth.
> Grant it; I still must envy them an age
> That favoured such a dream."

THE CULPRIT

*From fire, from water, and all things amiss,
Deliver the house of an honest justice.*

The Widow.

THE serenity of the Hall has been suddenly interrupted by a very important occurrence. In the course of this morning a posse of villagers was seen trooping up the avenue, with boys shouting in advance. As it drew near, we perceived Ready-Money Jack Tibbets striding along, wielding his cudgel in one hand, and with the other grasping the collar of a tall fellow, whom, on still nearer approach, we recognised for the redoubtable gipsy hero, Starlight Tom. He was now, however, completely cowed and crestfallen, and his courage seemed to have quailed in the iron grip of the lion-hearted Jack.

The whole gang of gipsy women and children came draggling in the rear; some in tears, others making a violent clamour about the ears of old Ready-Money, who, however, trudged on in silence with his prey, heeding their abuse as little as a hawk that has pounced upon a barn-door hero regards the outcries and cacklings of his whole feathered seraglio.

He had passed through the village on his way to the Hall, and of course had made a great sensation in that most excitable place, where every event is a matter of gaze and gossip. The report flew like wildfire that Starlight Tom was in custody. The ale-drinkers forthwith abandoned the tap-room; Slingsby's school broke loose, and master and boys swelled the tide that came rolling at the heels of old Ready-Money and his captive.

The uproar increased as they approached the Hall; it aroused the whole garrison of dogs, and the crew of hangers-on. The great mastiff barked from the dog-house; the stag-hound, and the grayhound, and the spaniel, issued barking from the Hall door, and my Lady Lillycraft's little dogs ramped

and barked from the parlour window. I remarked, however, that the gipsy dogs made no reply to all these menaces and insults, but crept close to the gang, looking round with a guilty, poaching air, and now and then glancing up a dubious eye to their owners; which shows that the moral dignity, even of dogs, may be ruined by bad company!

When the throng reached the front of the house, they

were brought to a halt by a kind of advanced guard, composed of old Christy, the gamekeeper, and two or three servants of the house, who had been brought out by the noise. The common herd of the village fell back with respect; the boys were driven back by Christy and his compeers; while Ready-Money Jack maintained his ground and his hold of the prisoner, and was surrounded by the tailor, the schoolmaster, and several other dignitaries of the village, and by the clamorous brood of gipsies, who were neither to be silenced nor intimidated.

By this time the whole household were brought to the doors and windows, and the Squire to the portal. An audience was demanded by Ready-Money Jack, who had detected the prisoner in the very act of sheep-stealing on his domains, and had borne him off to be examined before the Squire, who is in the commission of the peace.

A kind of tribunal was immediately held in the servants' hall, a large chamber with a stone floor and a long table in the centre, at one end of which, just under an enormous clock, was placed the Squire's chair of justice, while Master Simon took his place at the table as clerk of the court. An attempt had been made by old Christy to keep out the gipsy gang, but in vain; and they, with the village worthies, and the household, half filled the hall. The old housekeeper and the butler were in a panic at this dangerous irruption. They hurried away all the valuable things and portable articles that were at hand, and even kept a dragon watch on the gipsies, lest they should carry off the house clock or the deal table.

Old Christy, and his faithful coadjutor, the gamekeeper, acted as constables to guard the prisoner, triumphing in having at last got this terrible offender in their clutches. Indeed I am inclined to think the old man bore some peevish recollection of having been handled rather roughly by the gipsy in the chance-medley affair of May-day.

Silence was now commanded by Master Simon; but it was

'A kind of tribunal was immediately held in the servants' hall.'

difficult to be enforced in such a motley assemblage. There was a continued snarling and yelping of dogs, and, as fast as it was quelled in one corner, it broke out in another. The poor gipsy curs, who, like arrant thieves, could not hold up their heads in an honest house, were worried and insulted by the gentleman dogs of the establishment, without offering to make resistance ; the very curs of my Lady Lillycraft bullied them with impunity.

The examination was conducted with great mildness and indulgence by the Squire, partly from the kindness of his nature, and partly, I suspect, because his heart yearned towards the culprit, who had found great favour in his eyes, as I have already observed, from the skill he had at various times displayed in archery, morris-dancing, and other obsolete accomplishments. Proofs, however, were too strong. Ready-Money Jack told his story in a straightforward independent way, nothing daunted by the presence in which he found himself. He had suffered from various depredations on his sheep-fold and poultry-yard, and had at length kept watch, and caught the delinquent in the very act of making off with a sheep on his shoulders.

Tibbets was repeatedly interrupted, in the course of his testimony, by the culprit's mother, a furious old beldame, with an insufferable tongue, and who, in fact, was several times kept, with some difficulty, from flying at him tooth and nail. The wife, too, of the prisoner, whom I am told he does not beat above half a dozen times a week, completely interested Lady Lillycraft in her husband's behalf, by her tears and supplications ; and several other of the gipsy women were awakening strong sympathy among the young girls and maid-servants in the background. The pretty, black-eyed gipsy girl, whom I have mentioned on a former occasion as the sibyl that read the fortunes of the general, endeavoured to wheedle that doughty warrior into their interests, and even made some approaches to her old acquaintance, Master Simon; but was repelled by the latter, with all the dignity of office, having assumed a look of gravity and importance suitable to the occasion.

I was a little surprised, at first, to find honest Slingsby, the schoolmaster, rather opposed to his old crony Tibbets, and coming forwards as a kind of advocate for the accused. It seems that he had taken compassion on the forlorn fortunes of Starlight Tom, and had been trying his eloquence in his favour, the whole way from the village, but without effect. During the examination of Ready-Money Jack, Slingsby had stood like "dejected Pity at his side," seeking every now and then, by a soft word, to soothe any exacerbation of his ire, or to qualify any harsh expression. He now ventured to make a few observations to the Squire in palliation of the delinquent's offence; but poor Slingsby spoke more from the heart than the head, and was evidently actuated merely by a general sympathy for every poor devil in trouble, and a liberal toleration for all kinds of vagabond existence.

The ladies, too, large and small, with the kindheartedness of their sex, were zealous on the side of mercy, and interceded strenuously with the Squire; insomuch that the prisoner, finding himself unexpectedly surrounded by active friends, once more reared his crest, and seemed disposed for a time to put on the air of injured innocence. The Squire, however, with all his benevolence of heart, and his lurking weakness towards the prisoner, was too conscientious to swerve from the strict path of justice. There was abundant concurrent testimony that made the proof of guilt inconvertible, and Starlight Tom's mittimus was made out accordingly.

The sympathy of the ladies was now greater than ever; they even made some attempts to mollify the ire of Ready-Money Jack; but that sturdy potentate had been too much incensed by the repeated incursions that had been made into his territories by the predatory band of Starlight Tom, and he was resolved, he said, to drive the "varmint reptiles" out of the neighbourhood. To avoid all further importunities, as soon as the mittimus was made out, he girded up his loins, and strode back to his seat of empire, accompanied by his interceding friend, Slingsby, and followed by a detachment of the gipsy gang, who hung on his rear, assailing him with mingled prayers and execrations.

The question now was, how to dispose of the prisoner; a matter of great moment in this peaceful establishment, where

so formidable a character as Starlight Tom was like a hawk entrapped in a dovecot. As the hubbub and examination had occupied a considerable time, it was too late in the day to send him to the county prison, and that of the village was sadly out of repair from long want of occupation. Old Christy, who took great interest in the affair, proposed that the culprit should be committed for the night to an upper loft of a kind of tower in one of the outhouses, where he and the gamekeeper would mount guard. After much deliberation this measure was adopted; the premises in question were examined and made secure, and Christy and his trusty ally, the one armed with a fowling-piece, the other with an ancient blunderbuss, turned out as sentries to keep watch over this donjon-keep.

Such is the momentous affair that has just taken place, and it is an event of too great moment in this quiet little world, not to turn it completely topsy-turvy. Labour is at a stand. The house has been a scene of confusion the whole evening. It has been beleaguered by gipsy women, with their children on their backs, wailing and lamenting; while the old virago of a mother has cruised up and down the lawn in front, shaking her head and muttering to herself, or now and then breaking out into a paroxysm of rage, brandishing her fist at the Hall, and denouncing ill-luck upon Ready-Money Jack, and even upon the Squire himself.

Lady Lillycraft has given repeated audiences to the culprit's weeping wife, at the Hall door; and the servant-maids have stolen out to confer with the gipsy women under the trees. As to the little ladies of the family, they are all outrageous at Ready-Money Jack, whom they look upon in the light of a tyrannical giant of fairy tale. Phœbe Wilkins, contrary to her usual nature, is the only one that is pitiless in the affair. She thinks Mr. Tibbets quite in the right; and thinks the gipsies deserve to be punished severely for meddling with the sheep of the Tibbetses.

In the meantime the females of the family have evinced all the provident kindness of the sex, ever ready to soothe and succour the distressed, right or wrong. Lady Lillycraft has had a mattress taken to the outhouse, and comforts and delicacies of all kinds have been taken to the prisoner; even the little girls have sent their cakes and sweetmeats; so that,

I'll warrant, the vagabond has never fared so well in his life before. Old Christy, it is true, looks upon everything with a wary eye; struts about with his blunderbuss with the air of a veteran campaigner, and will hardly allow himself to be spoken to. The gipsy women dare not come within gunshot, and every tatterdemalion of a boy has been frightened from the park. The old fellow is determined to lodge Starlight Tom in prison with his own hands; and hopes, he says, to see one of the poaching crew made an example of.

I doubt, after all, whether the worthy Squire is not the greatest sufferer in the whole affair. His honourable sense of duty obliges him to be rigid, but the overflowing kindness of his nature makes this a grievous trouble to him.

He is not accustomed to have such demands upon his justice in his truly patriarchal domain; and it wounds his benevolent spirit, that, while prosperity and happiness are flowing in thus bounteously upon him, he should have to inflict misery upon a fellow-being.

He has been troubled and cast down the whole evening: took leave of the family, on going to bed, with a sigh, instead of his usual hearty and affectionate tone, and will, in all probability, have a far more sleepless night than his prisoner. Indeed this unlucky affair has cast a damp upon the whole household, as there appears to be an universal opinion that the unlucky culprit will come to the gallows.

Morning.—The clouds of last evening are all blown over. A load has been taken from the Squire's heart, and every face is once more in smiles. The gamekeeper made his appearance at an early hour, completely shamefaced and crestfallen. Starlight Tom had made his escape in the night; how he had got out of the loft no one could tell; the devil, they think, must have assisted him. Old Christy was so mortified that he would not show his face, but had shut himself up in his stronghold at the dog-kennel, and would not be spoken with. What has particularly relieved the Squire is, that there is very little likelihood of the culprit's being retaken, having gone off on one of the old gentleman's best hunters.

LOVERS' TROUBLES

The poor soul sat singing by a sycamore tree,
  Sing all a green willow;
Her hand on her bosom, her head on her knee,
  Sing willow, willow, willow;
Sing all a green willow must be my garland.

Old Song.

THE fair Julia having nearly recovered from the effects of her hawking disaster, it begins to be thought high time to appoint a day for the wedding. As every domestic event in a venerable and aristocratic family connection like this is a matter of moment, the fixing upon this important day has, of course, given rise to much conference and debate.

Some slight difficulties and demurs have lately sprung up, originating in the peculiar humours that are prevalent at the Hall. Thus, I have overheard a very solemn consultation between Lady Lillycraft, the parson, and Master Simon, as to whether the marriage ought not to be postponed until the coming month.

With all the charms of the flowery month of May, there is, I find, an ancient prejudice against it as a marrying month. An old proverb says, "To wed in May, is to wed poverty." Now, as Lady Lillycraft is very much given to believe in lucky and unlucky times and seasons, and indeed is very superstitious on all points relating to the tender passion, this old proverb seems to have taken great hold upon her mind. She recollects two or three instances in her own knowledge of matches that took place in this month, and proved very unfortunate. Indeed, an own cousin of hers, who married on a May-day, lost her husband by a fall from his horse, after they had lived happily together for twenty years.

The parson appeared to give great weight to her ladyship's objections, and acknowledged the existence of a prejudice of the kind, not merely confined to modern times, but prevalent likewise among the ancients. In confirmation of this, he quoted a passage from Ovid, which had a great effect on Lady Lillycraft, being given in a language which she did not understand. Even Master Simon was staggered by it; for he listened with a puzzled air, and then, shaking his head, sagaciously observed that Ovid was certainly a very wise man.

From this sage conference I likewise gathered several other important pieces of information relative to weddings; such as that if two were celebrated in the same church on the same day, the first would be happy, the second unfortunate. If, on going to church, the bridal party should meet the funeral of a female, it was an omen that the bride would die first; if of a male, the bridegroom. If the newly-married couple were to dance together on their wedding-day, the wife would thenceforth rule the roast; with many other curious and unquestionable facts of the same nature, all which made me ponder more than ever upon the perils which surround this happy state, and the thoughtless ignorance of mortals as to the awful risks they run in entering upon it. I abstain, however, from enlarging upon this topic, having no inclination to promote the increase of bachelors.

Notwithstanding the due weight which the Squire gives to traditional saws and ancient opinions, yet I am happy to find that he makes a firm stand for the credit of this loving month, and brings to his aid a whole legion of poetical authorities; all which, I presume, have been conclusive with the young couple, as I understand they are perfectly willing to marry in May, and abide the consequences. In a few days, therefore, the wedding is to take place, and the Hall is in a buzz of anticipation. The housekeeper is bustling about from morning till night, with a look full of business and importance, having a thousand arrangements to make, the Squire intending to keep open house on the occasion; and as to the housemaids, you cannot look one of them in the face, but the rogue begins to colour up and simper.

While, however, this leading love affair is going on with a tranquillity quite inconsistent with the rules of romance, I cannot say that the underplots are equally propitious. The "opening bud of love" between the general and Lady Lillycraft seems to have experienced some blight in the course of this genial season. I do not think the general has ever been able to retrieve the ground he lost when he fell asleep during the captain's story. Indeed, Master Simon thinks his case is completely desperate, her ladyship having determined that he is quite destitute of sentiment.

The season has been equally unpropitious to the love-lorn Phœbe Wilkins. I fear the reader will be impatient at having this humble amour so often alluded to; but I confess I am apt to take a great interest in the love troubles of simple girls of this class. Few people have an idea of the world of care and perplexity that these poor damsels have in managing the affairs of the heart.

We talk and write about the tender passion; we give it all

the colourings of sentiment and romance, and lay the scene of its influence in high life; but, after all, I doubt whether its sway is not more absolute among females of a humbler sphere. How often, could we but look into the heart, should we find the sentiment throbbing in all its violence in the bosom of the poor lady's maid, rather than in that of the brilliant beauty she is decking out for conquest; whose brain is probably bewildered with beaux, ball-rooms, and wax-light chandeliers.

With these humble beings love is an honest, engrossing concern. They have no ideas of settlements, establishments, equipages, and pin-money. The heart—the heart—is all-in-all

with them, poor things! There is seldom one of them but has her love cares, and love secrets; her doubts, and hopes, and fears, equal to those of any heroine of romance, and ten times as sincere. And then, too, there is her secret hoard of love documents;—the broken sixpence, the gilded brooch, the lock of hair, the unintelligible love scroll, all treasured up in her box of Sunday finery, for private contemplation.

How many crosses and trials is she exposed to from some

lynx-eyed dame, or staid old vestal of a mistress, who keeps a dragon watch over her virtue, and scouts the lover from the door! But then how sweet are the little love scenes, snatched at distant intervals of holiday, fondly dwelt on through many a long day of household labour and confinement! If in the country, it is the dance at the fair or wake, the interview in the churchyard after service, or the evening stroll in the green lane. If in town, it is perhaps merely a stolen moment of delicious talk between the bars of the area, fearful every instant of being seen ; and then, how lightly will the simple creature carol all day afterwards at her labour !

Poor baggage! after all her crosses and difficulties, when she marries, what is it but to exchange a life of comparative ease and comfort for one of toil and uncertainty ? Perhaps, too, the lover, for whom, in the fondness of her nature, she has committed herself to fortune's freaks, turns out a worthless churl, the dissolute, hard-hearted husband of low life ; who, taking to the alehouse, leaves her to a cheerless home, to labour, penury, and child-bearing.

When I see poor Phœbe going about with drooping eye, and her head hanging "all o' one side," I cannot help calling to mind the pathetic little picture drawn by Desdemona :—

> "My mother had a maid, called Barbara ;
> She was in love ; and he she loved proved mad
> And did forsake her ; she had a song of willow,
> An old thing 'twas ; but it expressed her fortune,
> And she died singing it."

I hope, however, that a better lot is in reserve for Phœbe Wilkins, and that she may yet "rule the roast" in the ancient empire of the Tibbetses! She is not fit to battle with hard hearts or hard times. She was, I am told, the pet of her poor mother, who was proud of the beauty of her child, and brought her up more tenderly than a village girl ought to be ; and ever since she has been left an orphan the good ladies at the Hall have completed the softening and spoiling of her.

I have recently observed her holding long conferences in the churchyard, and up and down one of the lanes near the village, with Slingsby the schoolmaster. I at first thought the pedagogue might be touched with the tender malady so prevalent in these parts of late; but I did him injustice. Honest Slingsby, it seems, was a friend and crony of her late father, the

parish clerk; and is on intimate terms with the Tibbets family. Prompted, therefore, by his good-will towards all parties, and secretly instigated, perhaps, by the managing Dame Tibbets, he has undertaken to talk with Phœbe upon the subject. He gives her, however, but little encouragement. Slingsby has a formidable opinion of the aristocratical feeling of old Ready-Money, and thinks, if Phœbe were even to make the matter up with the son, she would find the father totally hostile to the match. The poor damsel, therefore, is reduced almost to despair; and Slingsby, who is too good-natured not to sympathise in her distress, has advised her to give up all thoughts of young Jack, and has promised as a substitute his learned coadjutor, the prodigal son. He has even, in the fulness of his heart, offered to give up the school-house to them, though it would leave him once more adrift in the wide world.

THE WEDDING

No more, no more, much honour aye betide
The lofty bridegroom, and the lovely bride:
That all of their succeeding days may say.
Each day appears like to a wedding-day.

BRAITHWAITE.

NOTWITHSTANDING the doubts and demurs of Lady Lillycraft, and all the grave objections that were conjured up against the month of May, yet the Wedding has at length happily taken place. It was celebrated at the village church in presence of a numerous company of relatives and friends, and many of the tenantry. The Squire must needs have something of the old ceremonies observed on the occasion; so at the gate of the churchyard, several little girls of the village, dressed in white, were in readiness with baskets of flowers, which they strewed before the bride; and the butler bore before her the bride-cup, a great silver embossed bowl, one of the family reliques from the days of the hard drinkers. This was filled with rich wine, and decorated with a branch of rosemary, tied with gay ribands, according to ancient custom.

"Happy is the bride that the sun shines on," says the old proverb; and it was as sunny and auspicious a morning as heart could wish. The bride looked uncommonly beautiful; but, in fact, what woman does not look interesting on her wedding-day? I know no sight more charming and touching than that of a young and timid bride, in her robes of virgin white, led up trembling to the altar. When I thus behold a lovely girl, in the tenderness of her years, forsaking the house of her fathers and the home of her childhood, and, with the implicit, confiding, and the sweet self-abandonment which belong to woman, giving up all the world for the man of her choice; when I hear her, in the good old language of the ritual, yielding herself to him "for better for worse, for richer for poorer, in sickness and in health; to love, honour, and obey, till death us do part," it brings to my mind the beautiful and affecting self-devotion of Ruth:—"Whither thou goest I will go, and where thou lodgest I will lodge; thy people shall be my people, and thy God my God."

The fair Julia was supported on the trying occasion by Lady Lillycraft, whose heart was overflowing with its wonted sympathy in all matters of love and matrimony. As the bride approached the altar, her face would be one moment covered with blushes, and the next deadly pale; and she seemed almost ready to shrink from sight among her female companions.

I do not know what it is that makes every one serious, and, as it were, awestruck at a marriage ceremony, which is generally considered as an occasion of festivity and rejoicing. As the ceremony was performing, I observed many a rosy face among the country girls turn pale, and I did not see a smile throughout the church. The young ladies from the Hall were almost as much frightened as if it had been their own case, and stole many a look of sympathy at their trembling companion. A tear stood in the eye of the sensitive Lady Lillycraft; and as to Phœbe Wilkins, who was present, she absolutely wept and sobbed aloud; but it is hard to tell half the time what these fond, foolish creatures are crying about.

The captain, too, though naturally gay and unconcerned, was much agitated on the occasion, and, in attempting to put the ring upon the bride's finger dropped it on the floor; which Lady Lillycraft has since assured me is a very lucky omen. Even Master Simon had lost his usual vivacity, and had assumed a most whimsically solemn face, which he is apt to do on all occasions of ceremony. He had much whispering with the parson and parish clerk, for he is always a busy personage in the scene; and he echoed the clerk's amen with a solemnity and devotion that edified the whole assemblage.

The moment, however, that the ceremony was over, the transition was magical. The bride-cup was passed round, according to ancient usage, for the company to drink to a happy union; every one's feelings seemed to break forth from restraint: Master Simon had a world of bachelor pleasantries to utter, and as to the gallant general, he bowed and cooed about the dulcet Lady Lillycraft, like a mighty cock pigeon about his dame.

The villagers gathered in the churchyard to cheer the happy couple as they left the church; and the musical tailor had marshalled his band, and set up a hideous discord, as the blushing and smiling bride passed through a lane of honest peasantry to her carriage. The children shouted and threw up their hats; the bells rung a merry peel that set all the crows and rooks flying and cawing about the air, and threatened to bring down the battlements of the old tower; and there was a continual popping off of rusty firelocks from every part of the neighbourhood.

The prodigal son distinguished himself on the occasion, having hoisted a flag on the top of the school-house, and kept the village in a hubbub from sunrise with the sound of drum, and fife, and pandean pipe; in which species of music several

'The villagers gathered in the churchyard to cheer the happy couple.'

of his scholars are making wonderful proficiency. In his great zeal, however, he had nearly done mischief; for, on returning from church, the horses of the bride's carriage took fright from

the discharge of a row of old gun-barrels, which he had mounted as a park of artillery in front of the school-house, to give the captain a military salute as he passed.

The day passed off with great rustic rejoicings. Tables were spread under the trees in the park, where all the peasantry of the neighbourhood were regaled with roast beef and plum-pudding, and oceans of ale. Ready-Money Jack presided at one of the tables, and became so full of good cheer, as to unbend from his usual gravity, to sing a song out of all tune, and give two or three shouts of laughter, that almost electrified his neighbours, like so many peals of thunder. The schoolmaster and the apothecary vied with each other in making speeches over their liquor; and there were occasional glees and musical performances by the village band, that must have frightened every faun and dryad from the park. Even old Christy, who had got on a new dress, from top to toe, and shone in all the splendour of bright leather breeches, and an enormous wedding favour in his cap, forgot his usual crustiness, became inspired by wine and wassail, and absolutely danced a hornpipe on one of the tables, with all the grace and agility of a mannikin hung upon wires.

Equal gaiety reigned within doors, where a large party of friends were entertained. Every one laughed at his own pleasantry, without attending to that of his neighbours. Loads of bride-cake were distributed. The young ladies were all busy in passing morsels of it through the wedding ring to dream on, and I myself assisted a fine little boarding-school girl in putting up a quantity for her companions, which I have no doubt will set all the little heads in the school gadding, for a week at

least. After dinner all the company, great and small, gentle and simple, abandoned themselves to the dance: not the modern quadrille, with its graceful gravity, but the merry, social, old country dance: the true dance, as the Squire says, for a wedding occasion; as it sets all the world jigging in couples, hand in hand, and makes every eye and every heart dance merrily to the music. According to frank old usage, the gentlefolks of the Hall mingled, for a time, in the dance of the peasantry, who had a great tent erected for a ball-room; and I think I never saw Master Simon more in his element than when figuring about among his rustic admirers, as master of the ceremonies; and, with a mingled air of protection and gallantry, leading out the quondam Queen of May—all blushing at the signal honour conferred upon her.

In the evening the whole village was illuminated, excepting the house of the radical, who has not shown his face during the rejoicings. There was a display of fireworks at the school-house, got up by the prodigal son, which had well-nigh set fire to the building. The Squire is so much pleased with the extraordinary services of this last-mentioned worthy, that he talks of enrolling him in his list of valuable retainers, and promoting him to some important post on the estate; per-adventure to be falconer, if the hawks can ever be brought into proper training.

There is a well-known old proverb that says, "one wedding makes many"—or something to the same purpose; and I should not be surprised if it holds good in the present instance. I have seen several flirtations among the young people that have been brought together on this occasion; and a great deal of strolling about in pairs, among the retired walks and blossoming shrub-beries of the old garden; and if groves were really given to whispering, as poets would fain make us believe, Heaven knows what love-tales the grave-looking old trees about this venerable country-seat might blab to the world. The general, too, has waxed very zealous in his devotions within the last few days, as the time of her ladyship's departure approaches. I observed him casting many a tender look at her during the wedding dinner, while the courses were changing; though he was always liable to be interrupted in his adoration by the appearance of any new delicacy. The general, in fact, has arrived at that time of life when the heart and the stomach maintain a kind of balance of power; and when a man is apt to be perplexed in his affections between a fine woman and a truffled turkey. Her ladyship was certainly rivalled through the whole of the first course by a dish of stewed carp; and there was one glance, which was evidently intended to be a point-blank shot at her heart, and could scarcely have failed to effect a practicable breach, had it not unluckily been diverted away to a tempting breast of lamb, in which it immediately produced a formidable incision.

Thus did the faithless general go on, coqueting during the whole dinner, and committing an infidelity with every new dish; until, in the end, he was so overpowered by the attentions he had paid to fish, flesh, and fowl — to pastry, jelly, cream, and blanc-mange — that he seemed to sink within himself: his eyes swam beneath their lids, and their fire was so much slackened, that he could no longer discharge a single glance that would reach across the table. Upon the whole, I fear the general ate himself into as much disgrace, at this memorable dinner, as I have seen him sleep himself into on a former occasion.

I am told, moreover, that young Jack Tibbets was so touched by the wedding ceremony, at which he was present, and so captivated by the sensibility of poor Phœbe Wilkins, who certainly looked all the better for her tears, that he had a reconciliation with her that very day, after dinner, in one of the groves of the park, and danced with her in the evening, to the complete confusion of all Dame Tibbets' domestic politics. I met them walking together in the park, shortly after the reconciliation must have taken place. Young Jack carried himself gaily and manfully; but Phœbe hung her head, blushing, as I approached. However, just as she passed me, and dropped a curtsy, I caught a shy gleam of her eye from

under her bonnet; but it was immediately cast down again. I
saw enough in that single gleam, and in the involuntary smile
that dimpled about her rosy lips, to feel satisfied that the little
gipsy's heart was happy again.

What is more, Lady Lillycraft, with her usual benevolence and
zeal in all matters of this tender nature, on hearing of the recon-

ciliation of the lovers, undertook the critical task of breaking
the matter to Ready-Money Jack. She thought there was no
time like the present, and attacked the sturdy old yeoman that
very evening in the park, while his heart was yet lifted up with
the Squire's good cheer. Jack was a little surprised at being
drawn aside by her ladyship, but was not to be flurried by such
an honour; he was still more surprised by the nature of her
communication, and by this first intelligence of an affair that

had been passing under his eye. He listened, however, with his usual gravity, as her ladyship represented the advantages of the match, the good qualities of the girl, and the distress which she had lately suffered; at length his eye began to kindle, and his hand to play with the head of his cudgel. Lady Lillycraft saw that something in the narrative had gone wrong, and hastened to mollify his rising ire by reiterating the soft-hearted Phœbe's merit and fidelity, and her great unhappiness, when old Ready-Money suddenly interrupted her by exclaiming, that if Jack did not marry the wench, he'd break every bone in his body! The match, therefore, is considered a settled thing, Dame Tibbets and the housekeeper have made friends, and drunk tea together; and Phœbe has again recovered her good looks and good spirits, and is carolling from morning till night like a lark.

But the most whimsical caprice of Cupid is one that I should be almost afraid to mention, did I not know that I was writing for readers well acquainted in the waywardness of this most mischievous deity. The morning after the wedding, therefore, while Lady Lillycraft was making preparations for her departure, an audience was requested by her immaculate handmaid, Mrs. Hannah, who, with much priming of the mouth, and many maidenly hesitations, requested leave to stay behind, and that Lady Lillycraft would supply her place with some other servant. Her ladyship was astonished: "What! Hannah going to quit her, that had lived with her so long!"

"Why, one could not help it; one must settle in life some time or other." The good lady was still lost in amazement; at length the secret was gasped from the dry lips of the maiden gentlewoman; "she had been some time thinking of changing her condition, and at length had given her word, last evening, to Mr. Christy the huntsman."

How, or when, or where, this singular courtship had been carried on, I have not been able to learn; nor how she has been able, with the vinegar of her disposition, to soften the stony heart of old Nimrod; so, however, it is, and it has astonished every one. With all her ladyship's love of match-making, this last fume of Hymen's torch has been too much for her. She has endeavoured to reason with Mrs. Hannah, but all in vain; her mind was made up, and she grew tart on the least contradiction. Lady Lillycraft applied to the Squire for his interference. "She did not know what she should do without Mrs. Hannah, she had been used to have her about her so long a time."

The Squire, on the contrary, rejoiced in the match, as relieving the good lady from a kind of toilet-tyrant, under whose sway she had suffered for years. Instead of thwarting the affair, therefore, he has given it his full countenance; and declares that he will set up the young couple in one of the best cottages on his estate. The approbation of the Squire has been followed by that of the whole household; they all declare, that if ever matches are really made in heaven, this must have been; for that old Christy and Mrs. Hannah were as evidently formed to be linked together as ever were pepper-box and vinegar-cruet.

As soon as this matter was arranged, Lady Lillycraft took her leave of the family at the Hall; taking with her the captain and his blushing bride, who are to pass the honeymoon with her. Master Simon accompanied them on horseback, and indeed means to ride on ahead to make preparations. The general, who was fishing in vain for an invitation to her seat, handed her ladyship into her carriage with a heavy sigh; upon which his bosom friend, Master Simon, who was just mounting his horse, gave me a knowing wink, made an abominably wry face, and, leaning from his saddle, whispered loudly in my ear. 'It won't do!' Then putting spurs to his horse, away he cantered off. The general stood for some time waving his hat after the carriage as it rolled down the avenue, until he was seized with a fit of sneezing, from exposing his head to the cool breeze. I observed that he returned rather thoughtfully to the house; whistling thoughtfully to himself, with his hands behind his back, and an exceedingly dubious air.

The company have now almost all taken their departure. I have determined to do the same to-morrow morning; and I hope my reader may not think that I have already lingered too long at the Hall. I have been tempted to do so, however, because I thought I had lit upon one of the retired places where there are yet some traces to be met with of old English character.

A little while hence, and all these will probably have passed away. Ready-Money Jack will sleep with his fathers: the good Squire, and all his peculiarities, will be buried in the neighbouring church. The old Hall will be modernised into a fashionable country-seat, or, peradventure, a manufactory. The park will be cut up into petty farms and kitchen-gardens. A daily coach will run through the village; it will become, like all other commonplace villages, thronged with coachmen, post-boys, tipplers, and politicians; and Christmas, May-day, and all the other hearty merry-makings of the "good old times," will be forgotten.

Printed by R. & R. Clark, Edinburgh.

www.ingramcontent.com/pod-product-compliance
Lightning Source LLC
Chambersburg PA
CBHW031428230426
43668CB00007B/479